PENETRATING THE CAMPUS

REACHING KIDS WHERE THEY ARE

BARRY ST. CLAIR
AND
KEITH NAYLOR

ISBN 1-931617-24-4

1 2 3 4 5 6 7 8 9 10 Printing/Year 10 09 08 07 06 05 04 03 02

Produced in cooperation with Burt Stouffer, Stouffer Consulting and Ernest Pullen, Riverstone Group, LLC.

Printed in the United States of America

GETTING THE OVERALL PICTURE

OPENING COMMENTS

This book, as in any effort like this, became a reality because of a team effort. We, Barry and Keith, have a long relationship, having worked together on the staff of a church for eight years. A special thanks to attorney Marshall Albritton for writing virtually all of chapter 12. Your background gave this chapter the special legal expertise it needed. To Philip Brown, for your untiring efforts in reading our writing and working at the computer, we thank you. Finally, a word of appreciation to the Shawns, Julies, Antons, and all the other students who have inspired this book. You affirmed that kids really want to know Jesus!

Finally, let's clarify a few points. In *Penetrating the Campus* both of us relate several personal experiences. For simplicity's sake, our language style in this book represents both authors. Also, although we have taken pains to avoid stereotypes and generalizations, we have used masculine pronouns throughout to maintain stylistic consistency.

Barry St. Clair
Keith Naylor

SPECIAL HONOR

An expression of special honor goes to those people who inspired, motivated and equipped me with an ever-increasing passion for "the harvest."

Greg Simmons	Jack Stanton
Eric Nichols	Ken Chafin
Mal McSwain	Jack Taylor
Fred Crowell	Peter Lord
Mack Crenshaw	Buddy Price
Bill Bright	Walter St. Clair
Josh McDowell	Howard St. Clair

HOW TO MAXIMIZE THIS BOOK

Penetrating the Campus fits into an overall strategy to help you develop Jesus-focused youth ministry. Once a prayer strategy, a leadership team and discipleship groups with students are in place, then it is time to implement this book in your ministry.

Penetrating the Campus can reach its maximum potential in your ministry by using it in several beneficial ways. First, the youth leader can work on the book by himself. Second, he can pair up with other youth workers to discuss and implement the ideas presented in the book. Third, he can meet with his church youth workers to work through each chapter or section on a regular basis. Youth leaders will find helpful questions at the end of *Penetrating the Campus* to aid discussion.

Penetrating the Campus is designed for use with other resources that lay the foundation for Jesus-focused youth ministry.

Jesus-Focused Youth Ministry provides a self-training kit that gives you the pegs on which you can hang your entire ministry. We suggest that you go through this kit before you read and implement this book.

Building Leaders for Jesus-Focused Youth Ministry will equip your adult youth leaders to join you in penetrating the campus. We suggest that you start taking your leadership team through this before implementing *Penetrating the Campus*.

Moving Toward Maturity Series: This eight–book progressive discipleship series will move students to spiritual maturity in Christ.

Getting Started helps new believers successfully begin their walk with Christ.

Following Jesus builds a solid foundation for a life-changing relationship with Christ and for becoming a disciple of Christ.

Spending Time Alone with God deepens students' relationship with Jesus by learning how to spend time with Him.

Making Jesus Lord challenges students to obey Jesus and give Him control in the day-to-day issues they face.

Giving Away Your Faith guides students on the wild adventure of overcoming their fears and taking the risk to boldly communicate Christ.

Influencing Your World shows students that they can become influential leaders through serving the needs of the people around them.

Time Alone With God Notebook gives students practical tools for guiding them in their adventure with God.

Moving Toward Maturity Leader's Guide gives the group leader all that's needed to lead a lively and life-changing discipleship group. This book contains the leader's material for the five books that go through the discipleship process.

You can order these and other ministry resources:
www.reach-out.org 1-800-473-9456

PART ONE

CATCH GOD'S VISION FOR THE CAMPUS

ONE

OPEN YOUR EYES TO THE CAMPUS

"All I need is another thing to do."

As Gary and I talked over breakfast, I could sense that he had something more on his mind. A sharp youth leader who had served five years at a medium-sized, fast-growing church, Gary expressed frustration. "Something is missing. I have worked with some of the best students around. I have seen God do some tremendous things in my life and in the lives around me. But for the past six months I have been plagued with the question, 'Is what I'm doing really making an impact for Jesus Christ?'"

Youth leaders stay on the job an average of eighteen to twenty-four months. Many go to another church or "grow up and get a real job." They leave youth ministry for various reasons, but usually it's because they lack that burning purpose and direction that won't let them quit.

Purpose helps us know that what we do has value. It tells us, "You're using your life wisely." Direction gives us a sense of moving ahead. In youth ministry we can take many different directions, but all roads lead to Jesus Christ. Our purpose and direction has the focus of challenging young people to allow Jesus Christ to change their lives radically.

Most youth workers profess that their work is a noble calling. Standing in the gap, sacrificing our lives for students is the kind of work Jesus would do. But after we conduct our 300th youth meeting, endure our 20th lock-in, get stood up by the same student six times, and watch our houses get rolled every month just before it rains, we start to question our calling. We wonder if working in a sporting goods store would really be so bad. "Maybe all those people were right; maybe I do need to get a "real job" after all. Perhaps I should grow up and become part of the real world."

My friend Gary had come to this point. He expressed a longing to do more than serve as a glorified baby-sitter. He wanted to make an impact on the non-believing world for Jesus Christ. Gary discovered that 90 percent of all school-age children get their education in public schools.[1] The vast majority of these students do not know Jesus Christ. Most will never experience His love or hear the gospel unless someone goes to them. When Gary realized this, the lights came on. He knew his calling was to go!

Right now, you may be thinking, "Oh great, all I need is another responsibility to add to the thousand I have already." We agree that many good things can fill our calendars. But just because we're busy doesn't mean we're effective.

To get a clear perspective on our ministry purpose and direction, let's look at Jesus' pattern of ministry as recorded in Matthew 9:35-38:

> Jesus went through all the towns and villages, teaching in their synagogues, preaching the good news of the kingdom and healing every disease and sickness. When he saw the crowds, he had compassion on them, because they were *harassed* and *helpless*, *like sheep without a shepherd*. Then he said to his disciples, "The harvest is plentiful but the workers are few. Ask the Lord of the harvest, therefore, to send out workers into his harvest field" (Matthew 9:35-38, italics mine).

In that passage Jesus provides us with three reasons why we must go to the campus today.

JESUS WENT

In Matthew 9:35, we see that "Jesus went to all the towns and villages." Clearly, Jesus moved toward people; He did not expect people to come to Him. He deliberately chose a "go and tell" approach rather than a passive, laid-back "come and see" strategy. Like Jesus, we need that same "go and tell" approach. That way we will see "crowds" of people everywhere (v. 36). Because Jesus loved people, He went to them. He calls us to do the same.

Because Jesus loved people, He went to them. He calls us to do the same.

If you struggle with going, ask the Lord to do in you what He did with one youth leader. John had seen his youth group grow from six to one hundred students. One day, while meeting with his pastor, John bragged about all of the students he had brought into the youth group. Sensing his pride, the wise pastor said, "I'd like to show you something". They got into his car, drove to the local high school, and parked near the front entrance. The pastor instructed John to sit quietly and listen. All he could hear was the wind whispering softly through the trees and a few birds chirping in the distance. Suddenly, a ringing bell rudely interrupted the quietness. It was followed by the noise of hundreds of students walking out the front entrance of the school. The two men watched and listened. Some students came out laughing, but one was crying. Others talked with friends, but many walked alone. Lots of them yelled and screamed, and even a few cursed in anger, but others moved along quietly, not saying a word. Some acted arrogantly, while several showed fear. What they all had in common was a noticeable lack of purpose. They walked out the door without a clue about who to follow or where to go. For John, the picture his pastor painted for him that day was worth more than 10,000 words.

If we have not taken the gospel to the campus, we have come up short in fulfilling the mission that Jesus has given us, no matter how many students may come to the youth group. We must go because Jesus went.

A DESPERATE CAMPUS CULTURE

Matthew tells us, "When he saw the crowds, he had compassion on them, because they were harassed and helpless, like sheep without a shepherd" (Matthew 9:36). Matthew used three terms to identify the condition of the people: "harassed," "helpless," and "like sheep without a shepherd." The word harassed means "distressed, growing tired to the point of exhaustion"; picture in your mind a runner who has depleted his resources and has no more to give. Helpless conveys vulnerability. Such a person is thrown face down, like a person who is dead drunk and so incapacitated he can no longer defend himself. He has lost his will to decide for himself. And, "like sheep without a shepherd" indicates a lack of purpose and direction. Sheep put their faces in the grass and nibble wherever the grass takes them, with no purpose except the pleasure of the next moment. Many people are like that. As Jesus looked at the crowds, He recognized that they were exhausted, distressed, and purposeless. Similarly, the campus culture today finds itself harassed, helpless, and purposeless. This expresses itself in three significant and related areas.

EMOTIONALLY

Young people today find themselves forced into an adult environment without the time or the opportunity to grow up emotionally.

Young people today find themselves forced into an adult environment without the time or the opportunity to grow up emotionally.

They have to deal with problems that most adults experience difficulty handling, yet they rarely have the emotional maturity to do so. In 1987 Dr. Victor Stursberger of the American Academy of Pediatrics addressed this issue. The statement he made then holds true today:

> Short of being in a war, these are the most dangerous times adolescents have ever had to face. There are more choices teens have to make at younger ages and less guidance to make those choices. Now 14-15 year olds need to decide: "Am I going to have sex or not? Am I going to smoke pot or not? Am I going to drink or not?" Two generations ago those decisions were made in college. A generation ago they were made in high school. Now they are being made in junior high.[2]

Furthermore, in an environment consumed with self, young people have no protective safeguard of love to fall back on when they fail. Every thirteen seconds another set of parents gets divorced.[3] Divorce has profoundly negative effects on children. Compared to children from intact homes, children of divorce are far more likely to struggle academically, engage in drug and alcohol use and other high-risk behaviors, commit suicide, experience psychiatric problems, and live in poverty. Thirty years of research now conclusively shows that divorce is harmful to children in virtually every measure.[4] The children become the support system for the single parent. Often they become a human weapon that one parent uses to attack the other; they feel forced to take sides. After a fifteen-year-old friend had just told me about his parents deciding to divorce, he prayed, "God, I pray that my parents won't break up so I won't have to choose."

In 2000, an estimated 879,000 children in the U. S. were victims of abuse or neglect, a rate of 12.2 per 1,000 children under 18.[5] Each day in the United States, more than three children die as a result of child abuse in the home. Approximately three million child abuse reports are made each year. Child abuse is reported — on average — every ten seconds. Nearly one-half of substantiated cases of child neglect and abuse are associated with parental alcohol or drug abuse.[6]

The normal emotional turmoil of adolescence poses difficult problems in itself. But combined with living in the atmosphere just described, the strain can turn the young person into an emotional cripple, unable to handle normal teenage pressures. According to the American Journal of Psychiatry, the teen years are the most common age for depression. About 12 million children under 18 suffer from mental disorders such as autism, depression, and hyperactivity. They feel emotionally empty and therefore see life as an endless series of problems.[7]

SOCIALLY

The emotional distress of students leads them on a search to find a way to fill the emptiness inside. Like other people, students want to experience love. Yet, young people fear that they will not have the opportunity to love or be loved.

Young people fear that they will not have the opportunity to love or be loved.

Most young people who come from an emotionally crippled background will have a distorted view of love. To them, love means sexual involvement, and love's ultimate expression is sexual contact. Statistics bear this out. By their 18th birthday, 6 in 10 teenage women and nearly 7 in 10 teenage men have had sexual intercourse.[8] Nationwide, 6.6 percent of students reported initiating sexual intercourse before age 13.[9]

Most students believe they will find love when they experience sex. Often, however, they miss out on the love they so deeply desire. In fact, their sexual activity leads them into greater insecurity. Their fear of not being loved intensifies and is eventually realized as the sexual relationship disintegrates. Not only do they lose the love they searched for, but they become alienated from and hurt by the people they thought loved them.

Nearly one million teen girls get pregnant each year. Nearly 4 out of 10 young women get pregnant at least once before they turn 20. Each year the federal government alone spends about $40 billion to help families that began with a teenage birth.[10]

EVERY 24 HOURS . . .

17,297	public school students are suspended.*
7,883	children are reported abused or neglected.
4,248	children are arrested.
3,585	babies are born to unmarried mothers.
2,861	high school students drop out.
2,319	babies are born to mothers who are not high school graduates.
2,019	babies are born into poverty.
1,329	babies are born to teen mothers.
1,310	babies are born without health insurance.
825	babies are born at low birth weight (less than 5 lbs., 8 oz.).
401	babies are born to mothers who had late or no prenatal care.
367	children are arrested for drug abuse.
180	children are arrested for violent crimes.
157	babies are born at very low birth weight (less than 3 lbs., 4 oz.).
77	babies die.
34	children and youth under 20 from accidents.
9	children or youth under 20 die from firearms.
9	children or youth under 20 are homicide victims.
5	children or youth under 20 commit suicide.
1	young person under 25 dies from HIV infection.[11]

Today when teenagers become one of these statistics, instead of receiving more love, they often loses the love they thought they had.

Many make the unwise choice to have an abortion. The highest abortion rate among all women is among 18 to 19 year old women - 56 percent per 1,000 women.[12] While abortion seems to be a way out of the intense social pressures that a teen faces with pregnancy, it results instead in inner turmoil. Eighty-one percent of the teens who have abortions become preoccupied with the death of that child afterwards. Seventy-three percent had flashbacks of the abortion experience, 69% experienced feelings of "craziness" and 54% had nightmares related to the abortion. Thirty-five percent perceived a visitation from the aborted child and 23% had hallucinations related to the abortion.[13] One nineteen-year-old rape victim who terminated her pregnancy said,

> I felt an emptiness that nothing could fill, and quickly discovered that the aftermath of abortion continued a long time after the memory of the rape dimmed. For the next three years I experienced horrible depression and nightmares. I dreamed I was giving birth, but they would take my baby away from me. I'd hear her crying and I'd search but I couldn't find her anywhere. I'd just hear her cries echoing in the distance.[14]

Students like this feel socially bankrupt and unable to carry on sustained relationships.

SPIRITUALLY

Adding to their emotional and social distress, teenagers live in an environment that not only offers no real hope, but even adds to their problems. The average high school graduate has spent 18,720 hours in his twelve years on the campus, excluding extracurricular activities. Those years are spent in an atmosphere that teaches a philosophy of life with no absolutes. In the age of science and technology, they think that life is related not to an all-powerful, all-knowing God, but revolves only around themselves.

That philosophy and the resulting classroom atmosphere often robs students in public schools of true education. Students rarely have the opportunity to seek answers that can meet their real-life needs. Most of the time they aren't even given the privilege of considering the possibility that God can fill the emptiness in their hearts.

Because high school students sense no relief from the emptiness of their culture, they do what seems logical—they quit trying. At school they hear, "You came from nothing and you are going to nothing." They conclude quickly that everything in between means nothing. One bumper sticker summarized the hopelessness students feel: "Life's a Bitch, Then You Die." Not surprisingly, many of today's students have given up. They see no hope.

When hopelessness prevails over a period of time, students try to escape. Ninety-two percent of our young people have taken a drink of alcohol at least once. The average age when youth first try alcohol is 11 years of age for boys and 13 years of age for girls.[15] Many students are so desperate to escape that they will try any-thing, including sniffing Scotchgard™ and other inhalants. It has been estimated that over three million teenagers are out-and-out alcoholics. Several million more have a serious drinking problem that they cannot manage on their own.[16]

The severity of hopelessness causes some to choose a permanent escape. Suicide among young people has nearly tripled since the 1950's. Today it is the third lead-ing cause of death among teens, behind accidents and homicide.[17] The suicide rate among children ages 10-14 was 1.2/100,000. The suicide rate among adoles-cents aged 15-19 was 8.2/100,000. Among young people 20-24 years of age the suicide rate was 12.7/100,000.[18]

Today we have the most reckless society of youth ever. Violence causes 8 out of 10 deaths among adolescents and has passed disease as the leading cause of mortal-ity among young people. Violence (homicide and suicide) accounts for 40% of ado-lescent deaths. Homicide is the second leading killer and suicide is the third leading cause of death for youth, ages 15 to 24, in the United States.[19] For 10 – 14-year-olds, firearm-related violence is the third leading cause of death. Firearm-related homicide is the second leading cause of death among young Americans 15 to 19 years of age.[20] Campus shootings have become commonplace.

Obviously, students want a reason to live! But only Jesus gives a reason to live. He is the only one who holds the answer for "the harassed, the helpless, the sheep with-out a shepherd."

THE LABORERS ARE FEW

Jesus recognized that the harvest was "plentiful," that the people were ripe to expe-rience love, fulfillment, peace, and hope from God. They were searching for something worth living for, and even more important, something worth dying for.

In the same way, young people today are searching. Personally, I have never seen a time when so many students are so open to the gospel of Christ. One day a young girl I had met on campus handed me a note. It read:

> Lately my life has been crazy. Everything seems to be going wrong. . . . Still I wish I had someone I could talk to. That's mostly why I was hoping we could still find a way to get together.

This young girl's family never went to church, and her parents had each been through at least one divorce after they divorced. She had never heard that God loved her and that she could have a relationship with Him. Three weeks after she handed me the note, she accepted Christ through another student involved in our ministry.

Students are searching frantically, desperately. They want to know if they can trust anyone, if anyone cares, if anyone is real.

Students want to know if love and commitment are just words or something they can truly experience.

One of the primary reasons young people have premarital sex is because they long for love or anything that resembles it. They also wonder if God really exists and if He can love them just the way they are.

But if students keep coming up empty handed, it's because very few people make themselves available to share the unconditional love of God with them. We have spent a combined total of more than thirty years on the campus, yet we have encountered very few youth workers in that time. In a ten-year period only five other youth workers visited our campus. Two of those were Mormon missionaries.

It is frequently said that a high school student will have only a 15 percent chance of accepting Christ later in life if he hasn't done so before graduation. In light of that, Jesus' statement in John 20:21 makes great sense: "As the Father has sent me, I am sending you."

God wants to use you to bring the love of Christ to the campus. Will you go?

TAKING ACTION

The "Open Your Eyes" Strategy

1. In your work with young people, when have you been frustrated by your inability to make the kind of impact you want to make? Identify one or two specific frustrations.

_____

_____

_____

2. As you read through Matthew 9:35-38 thoughtfully, describe why you think Jesus "went" through all the towns and villages.

_____

_____

3. From what you learned in this chapter, why is it important for you to go? Give at least three reasons.

_____

_____

_____

4. Give a specific description of how students you know feel harassed, helpless, and like sheep without a shepherd in each of the areas listed below. Ask the Lord to help you identify with what they feel.

Emotionally:

_____

_____

Socially:

Spiritually:

5. Imagine that Jesus came to visit your local campus. Why would He tell you "the harvest is plentiful" there?

6. Why would Jesus say "the laborers are few" in talking about your campus?

7. When Jesus says, "Ask the Lord of the harvest, therefore, to send out workers into his harvest field," how do you think that statement applies to your local situation?

8. From what you have discovered in this chapter, what is the one compelling reason that will motivate you to go to the campus?

_____

_____

_____

9. After praying about this question every day for a week, answer the question, "Will I go?" Record your response below.

_____

_____

_____

NOTES

1. Forrest L. Turpin, "Salt in the Public School," Voices (Pasadena, Calif.: Christian Educators Assoc. Intl.), 4-5.

2. Dr. Victor I. Stursberger, "Today's Adolescents-Different Choices, Greater Risks," *Youthworker Update*, vol. 1, no. 6 (Feb. 1987), 1.

3. Divorce Resource Network. 2001-2002. <http://www.divorceresourcenetwork.org/> (December, 2002)

4. Focus on the Family – Citizen Link. *Divorce and Public Policy Fact Sheet* by Amy Desai, J. D., 2001, <http://www.family.org/cforum/research/papers/a001618.html> (December, 2002)

5. Maternal and Child Health Bureau/Child Health USA 2002. <http://www.mchb.hrsa.gov/chusa02/main_pages/page_06.htm> (December, 2002)

6. Childhelp USA" Childabuse.com/, March 2002, <www.childabuse.com/newsletter/stat0301.htm>

7. Friends Hospital, Facts About Mental Illness, <www.friendshospitalonline.org/facts.htm> (December, 2002)

8. The Alan Guttmacher Institute, *Facts in Brief: Sexuality Education*, <http://www.guttmacher.org/pubs/fb_sex_ed02.html> (December, 2002)

9. Advocates For Youth, Katie Dillard, *Adolescent Sexual Behavior I: Demographics,* November, 2002 <http://www.advocatesforyouth.org/publications/factsheet/fsbehdem.htm> (December, 2002)

10. National Campaign To Prevent Teen Pregnancy, <http://www.teenpregnancy.org/resources/teensfacts/fact1.asp> (December, 2002)

11. Children's Defense Fund, <http://www.childrensdefense.org/everyday.htm> (December, 2002)

12. Focus on the Family – Crisis Pregnancy Ministry, *The Status of Abortion in America* <http://www.family.org/pregnancy/general/A0014243.html> (December, 2002)

13. Pro-Life America <http://www.prolife.com/ABORT12.html> (December, 2002)

14. Sharon Bennett, "Three Victims of Rape," *Americans Against Abortion* (Last DaysMinistries), vol. 1, no. 2 (Summer 1986), 8.

15. Focus Adolescent Services, *Alcohol and Teen Drinking* <http://www.focusas.com/Alcohol.html> (December, 2002)

16. Focus Adolescent Services, *Alcohol and Teen Drinking* <http://www.focusas.com/Alcohol.html> (December, 2002)

17. Suicide & Crisis Center, *Suicide Facts & Statistics* <http://www.sccenter.org/facts.html> (December, 2002)

18. National Institute of Mental Health, Suicide Facts <http://www.nimh.nih.gov/research/suifact.htm> (December, 2002)

19. Focus Adolescent Service, *Teen Violence* <http://www.focusas.com/Violence.html> (December, 2002)

20. Focus Adolescent Service, *Teen Violence* <http://www.focusas.com/Violence.html> (December, 2002)

TWO

PREPARE YOUR HEART

"Does someone like me really qualify?"

Slowly I approached the campus. My heart jumped with anticipation as I thought about what God could do through me there.

I located the gym! Here I would find success. I understood the value students put on athletics. I had spent my life playing basketball. In the best shape of my life, I had a wide variety of slam dunks (well, actually two). With a brand new pair of top-notch athletic shoes, my NBA pro-am basketball shorts, and a tan that every guy would envy, I said to myself, "It's time to rescue these poor heathen from destruction." I knew that when they saw my incredible athletic ability, I would gain the respect needed to have a successful ministry on campus. I picked the biggest guy on the court and challenged him to a game of one-on-one. As I had hoped, the game quickly drew a crowd. I proceeded to humiliate the guy in front of everyone.

The game finished in record time. I walked to the side of the court to receive the admiration that I anticipated from the crowd. Not only did the guy I beat not want to talk to me, but no one else hung around either. That experience deflated my ego and caused me to rethink my approach, not to mention my motives!

What, then, does it take for personal effectiveness on the campus? Do I have to have good looks? Tell great jokes? Play the guitar? Drive a hot, new sports car? Have athletic ability? Dress weird? Have long hair? Or short hair? And if I have evolved into an out-of-touch nerd over the years, can God still use me? What does it take? The qualification for success on the campus: LOVE!

The qualification for success on the campus: LOVE!

Unconditional love! Pure, unadulterated love that needs no dressing up to keep up with the times. With God's love anyone can minister to students. And the possibilities for ministry become limitless through a person who can love as Christ loves.

Realizing that, how can we adjust to God's approach in reaching kids? Let's look at two sides of the same coin: (1) we must be capable of love, and (2) we must be compelled by love.

CAPABLE OF LOVE

The stark contrast between a Christian and a non-Christian rests upon our God-given ability to love unconditionally. We find the clue to this in God's nature expressed in John 3:16. Jesus said, "For God so loved the world that he gave..." *Vine's Expository Dictionary* defines the Greek word for love *(agapao)* as the "deep and constant love of a perfect being toward entirely unworthy objects." God's supernatural love receives the other person unconditionally in spite of attitudes, actions, and behavior. If he swears, tells off-color jokes, takes drugs, drinks, moons your youth group (which has actually happened), or even makes fun of Jesus Christ, agape love receives that person with no strings attached.

Only God can express that kind of love. He has chosen not only to express that love to us, but also to give us the capability to pass that love along to others.

If you are like me, you probably are saying, "I struggle with love—receiving it and giving it." So what does the Lord want to do in us to expand our capacity to love?

In 1 Timothy 1:5 we receive clear instructions on how we can love students unconditionally. Paul said, "The goal of this command is love, which comes from a pure heart and a good conscience and a sincere faith." How do I become a channel of God's love?

A PURE HEART

A person with a *pure* heart, according to that word's original Greek meaning, has a heart that is *clean* and *complete*. A pure heart becomes clean when a person confesses his sins. Picture *clean* as a spotless dish. If you leave the cereal bowl by the sink in the sun all day, you will need an air hammer to get the cereal off by evening. How much better to wash the bowl as soon as it gets dirty. That's the idea here. Sensitively, honestly, eagerly, and quickly deal with all sin.

For years I participated in an aggressive ministry that shared the gospel of Christ through athletics. Yet at the same time I struggled daily with lust. I would share the love of Jesus with thousands of people one night, then the next I would watch a sex-saturated movie. Miserable, I hated myself and my hypocrisy. I would cry out to God, but all the while I kept my struggle to myself. Finally, when I could stand it no more, I opened my heart to another brother in Christ. For the first time I confessed all my sin to God before another person. God forgave me. He cleansed me. Within a brief time, I was set free from all the problems that entangled me. In the midst of this I realized that my biggest sin was not lust at all, but pride. My desire to protect my reputation was greater than my desire to come clean with God. When I got to the point in my life where I said, "Father, being in Your presence is more important than what anyone thinks of me," then He set me free. It's wonderful to be clean! Not perfect, but clean!

Are you more concerned with what you look like on the outside than with who you are on the inside? Do you have sins hidden in your life? Are you an imposter? The writer of Proverbs spoke clearly to this issue: "He who conceals his sins does not prosper, but whoever confesses and renounces them finds mercy" (Proverbs 28:13). God uses people who have clean hearts, who have "cleaned the dish", who honestly confess their sins to God.

Second, a person with a pure heart has a *complete* heart. That means he has a single-minded focus. A single-minded person has unmixed motives. Jesus Christ has become his total motivation, purpose, and goal. He wants Jesus to control his mind, his heart, his activities, and his time. He willingly lets go of good things in life in order to pursue God's best.

Such a person was Count Nicolaus Ludwig von Zinzendorf. This young, intelligent, eighteenth-century German leader put it this way: "I have but one passion. It is He. He alone."

"I have but one passion. It is He. He alone."

It was the single-minded passion of Count Zinzendorf that provided the motivation for the Moravian movement to send out more missionaries than anyone else in the eighteenth century. It was that passion for God that caused the Lord to use Count Zinzendorf to disciple Peter Böhler, who witnessed to John Wesley, which led directly to Wesley having his heart "strangely warmed" at Aldersgate. It was Zinzendorf's passion for God that allowed the Lord to use him to start a prayer meeting that lasted 24 hours a day for 100 years.

Now more than ever, students need to know that Jesus is real. And they will see that reality in your passion for God. What is preventing you from pursuing a pure heart?

A GOOD CONSCIENCE

In order for God's love to flow to young people through an unclogged, free-flowing channel, you need a "good conscience." This means that all of your relationships with others need to be in order. That means, with both Christians and non-Christians, you do everything you can to make right any wrong relationships, including those with parents, brothers and sisters, children, pastors, people at church, friends, former friends, and spouse. Not everyone will accept your offer, and you still may have enemies. But you will imitate Paul's example in Acts 24:16: "So I strive always to keep my conscience clear before God and man."

What steps do I take to have a good conscience? First, have you released and forgiven any grudge, anger, or resentment toward another person? (See Matthew 18:15-16.) Second, if you have wronged someone else, have you asked his forgiveness? (See Matthew 5:23-24.) Can you say with confidence, "I have no broken relationships because I have both forgiven others and asked others' forgiveness"?

Once I had a hard time getting along with my basketball coach. This bugged me because it seemed inconsistent with our team's goal of sharing Christ with others. It didn't seem right to say "God loves you and so do I" when I couldn't even love my coach.

For four years I struggled with these feelings. I felt that my unhappiness was the coach's fault and so I didn't try to get matters right. I avoided him when I could and tolerated him when I had to. I talked about him behind his back. Several other players did the same. We would have "rip sessions." In other words, we would verbally rip him apart among ourselves. Then we validated our actions with the argument that he was the one who was wrong.

When I left the team, I thought, *Finally I am free from him. I don't have to deal with him anymore.* About a year later, after I read 1 Timothy 1:5, God showed me how wrongly I had responded and showed me that I needed to make the relationship right with my former coach.

Yet I rationalized: *I haven't seen him in a year. I'll probably never see him again anyway. He probably didn't notice my feelings toward him.* I thought of more and more excuses, but to no avail. God had spoken. I had only two choices: to obey or to disobey. I decided to obey. I called my coach and asked for his forgiveness. When I called I said, "Coach, I was wrong in the way I handled my relationship with you." Then I listed everything I had done to hurt him. After that I said "Will you forgive me?" He did!

John tells us, "If anyone says, 'I love God,' yet hates his brother, he is a liar. For anyone who does not love his brother, whom he has seen, cannot love God, whom he has not seen" (1 John 4:20). I saw that if I did not love my coach, then I really didn't love God either. In order to open the channel of God's unconditional love to others, including students, we need to make all of our relationships right. Have you done that?

A SINCERE FAITH

A sincere faith opens up the spigot of God's unconditional love and allows it to flow through us. The Greek word translated as "sincere" means literally "without hypocrisy." It speaks of a person who lives a real, true faith. This kind of person not only believes, but what he believes he lives out consistently.

Depression and low self-esteem plague our society. Often depression and low self-esteem come from not living up to what we know is right and to what we believe. We start living a lie. Don't misunderstand. The emphasis here is not so much on making our lives match our words, but rather on making our words match our lives.

The ancient Greeks would have likened a sincere person to a sculpture "without wax." In those days a sculptor would come to town and carve out a statue. A person would buy it. Sometimes a less-skilled and devious sculptor would hide his mistakes. He might accidentally chip off a piece of a nose or elbow. Then the crook would patch the sculpture with wax and sell it as authentic. He was dishonest, insincere.

You need no longer build your self-esteem on who you appear to be. Because you are unconditionally loved by God, you, as His beloved, can be who you are. Quite simply, you are of great value to God, precious in His sight, just because you are you! God wants you to express that honest, "I am who I am" sincerity before Him and before others around you. He wants you to live "without wax."

Listening to the speaker at a conference I had set up, I realized that my obedience did not measure up to my knowledge. One particular issue always came to mind when sin was mentioned. As the Lord lovingly brought this matter to my attention, I realized that either I had to obey or God wasn't going to use me anymore. That scared me. But to deal with it also scared me. I had cheated on some German tests in college. I knew that I had disobeyed God then, and that I was disobeying Him now by not facing that professor. I didn't want to confront this problem because I knew the results would be devastating. What a struggle! Finally I decided to obey God. I've never been so nervous as the day I stepped into my office to call that professor and get things right. I asked him to forgive me for cheating in his class. He could have taken away my degree but instead he forgave me. When it was over I was free! And that incident has never been an issue since.

When we live in the reality that we are loved by God, then we are free to be ourselves and free to please Him through honest, sincere obedience. A friend put it this way: "You put into practice what you believe every day. All the rest is just religious talk."

"You put into practice what you believe every day. All the rest is just religious talk."

A sincere faith spurs us on to obey Jesus Christ totally.

The greatest mistake people can make in trying to penetrate the campus is thinking they can love students even though their own "love channel" is clogged. But when a person desires a pure heart, a good conscience, and sincere faith, then love flows. We become open channels pouring out God's unconditional love on young people. Then the possibilities on the campus are limitless!

COMPELLED BY LOVE

As I stumbled through the kitchen, I glanced at the clock. It was 1:00 AM. I clumsily grabbed the phone off the hook, trying desperately to figure out where I was and who would be calling me at this time of the night. I cleared my throat and gave my best attempt at "hello." On the other end, the mother of one of the girls in my youth group spoke frantically. She asked if I would come over to her house and talk to Rob, a young man who was dating her daughter. Rob attended the youth group. He had been dramatically converted to Christ two years before. For two years I had poured my life into him. I had gotten closer to Rob than to any other student.

But that night Rob had lost it. Pam (the daughter of the lady who called) had broken off the relationship with Rob. He came to Pam's house angry and drunk. When I went to the house, I found Rob out of control.

After several hours of talking, I concluded that talking wouldn't help the situation. I told him he had three options: to go home, to go to the hospital, or to have the police come for him. It was his choice. Rob decided to go home.

I haven't seen Rob since. He turned completely away from God. He won't talk to me. He told others that I betrayed him and that he never wants to see me again. For several weeks that experience devastated me. Because we had a strong friendship, hardly a day goes by that my heart doesn't hurt because of Rob. But equally traumatic was the confusion and disappointment I felt because Rob had turned away from God.

Because disappointments like this are common in campus ministry, something deeper, something stronger has to carry us through the rejections we will face. Only one thing will give us the determination and endurance not to give up. It's the same thing that gave Christ the strength He needed to die on the cross for a world that rejected Him—the love of God. We find in 2 Corinthians 5:14 a clear expression of how such love can influence us: "For Christ's love compels us. . ."

Realizing how much we are loved by Christ motivates us to give our lives away to others. It also sustains us through the difficult times. In 2 Corinthians 4:8-10, the Apostle Paul writes,

We are hard pressed on every side, but not crushed; perplexed, but not in despair; persecuted, but not abandoned; struck down, but not destroyed. We always carry around in our body the death of Jesus, so that the life of Jesus may also be revealed in our body.

A person who ministers over the long haul on the campus is sustained by the example of Christ's love demonstrated on the cross. Even if people don't respond and we don't feel successful, with that kind of love flowing in and through us we can press forward to love kids unconditionally. Let's look at some practical ways to release that love to students.

1. *Focus on Spiritual Reality.* Daily our world bombards us with the lie that the important things in life are what we own, what we drive, how we look, and what we eat. We get the false impression that reality exists only in the physical world, that is, what we can see and touch.

But God tells us that the physical fades away. The spiritual world is all that will last forever. It is the "real reality." God wants to continually remind us: "Set your hearts on things above, where Christ is seated at the right hand of God. Set your minds on things above, not on earthly things" (Colossians 3:2). When our hearts are set on the Lord and His concerns, then we can live from the perspective that everything we do will last for eternity. Whether leading a student to Christ or continuing to love a student who has shunned us for the one-hundredth time, we are building up treasures in heaven that will last forever.

> When our hearts are set on the Lord and His concerns, then we can live from the perspective that everything we do will last for eternity.

Paul encourages us, "Let us not become weary in doing good, for at the proper time we will reap a harvest if we do not give up" (Galatians 6:9). We can do that because everything we do in the name of Christ—every kind word, sacrifice, pat on the back, meeting with an apathetic kid, act of service—will bring an eternal reward when Jesus comes in all of His glory. That perspective can compel us to continue to love.

2. *Enjoy the Journey.* A friend, flying to his destination and trying to get his work done, kept getting interrupted by a sweet little old lady. He answered her questions

politely but gave no opportunity to continue the conversation. Obviously she was an intrusion to him. The interruptions got more annoying as the plane moved closer to its destination. As the plane taxied to the gate, the little old lady, sensing his agitation, leaned over to him and said, "Honey, if you can't enjoy the journey, then what good is the destination?"

Often, as we go through life, we set goals and then become so focused on those goals that we can't see anything else except those goals. For example, it's easy to envision hundreds of students coming to Christ. That's wonderful unless each student becomes an "objective" to help us achieve that goal. Then our faulty thinking becomes: "If one student doesn't quite fit, forget him. Move on to the next one." Suddenly these goals control our lives rather than our lives controlling the goals. Jesus never ministered in this way. He enjoyed the process. Unhurried, He took the time to love children, to stay over with the Samaritans, and to hang out with Zacchaeus. He focused on the needs at hand without worrying about what else He had to do.

Understand that each time we walk on campus, each time we encounter a student, that encounter is a divine appointment. Knowing this gives us God's perspective. It helps take the pressure off. We can sit back and watch God work without being anxious about winning the entire school to Christ. Do you enjoy the journey? The love of Christ compels us to do so.

3. Embrace Difficulties Enthusiastically. Whatever difficult circumstances surround your life right now, God wants to use them to expand your capacity to love. Once, a desperate mom begged me for advice on how to help her son. He had recently been in jail for drug abuse, for stealing, and for threatening to kill her and her husband. She told me that everyone she knew was praying for her son. I pointed out that maybe she needed to have these people pray for her. That remark confused her. Wasn't her son the one who needed help? I tried to help her see that God might want to change her more than her son by allowing these tough circumstances to happen. Maybe God was using her son's difficulties to bring her to a greater awareness of His purpose for her life.

We can apply this reality to our work with kids. God loves them more than we do. Still sometimes we wonder: God, why are You not changing them more quickly? Correctly, the more we love them, the more we agonize over them. But remember, God not only wants to change them, He wants to change us as well.

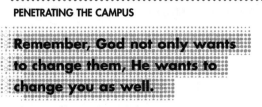

Remember, God not only wants to change them, He wants to change you as well.

As you minister to students who break your heart, remember that God uses them to enlarge your capacity to love and to compel you to love even more. Right now, will you embrace your difficult circumstances so God can change you?

4. Spread the Love to Lost Students. God's love in our lives encourages us to give our greatest effort to reach lost kids with the message of that same love. The more we enter into relationships with non-Christians, the greater our burden for them will become. They desperately need the love of Christ.

During a discussion in my living room I asked a group of students the question, "If you could have one thing in life what would it be?" Jessica spoke up first. She said, "I would have a mom." Then she broke down and cried. She told us that when she was eight years old, her mom had died. Another family had adopted her. Since then she had lost two moms through divorce, and she currently had no mom. Only because of her dad had she not killed herself. "All I ever wanted was a mom I could talk to and who would hold me."

Another time after a youth meeting Tommy grabbed me. He wanted to talk about God. Tommy, his sister, and his two brothers had been raised by his mother since he was twelve. Tommy's dad left when he found out Tommy's little brother had Down's Syndrome. Tommy didn't like to talk about his dad. And he got into a lot of fights at school. Most of the time he seemed angry. Never in his life had Tommy gone to church. But that night Tommy accepted Christ. At the end of our conversation he looked me in the eye and said, "This is the first time my heart has ever felt clean."

Only through intimate involvement in young peoples' lives will we be able to apply the love of Christ to the thousands of kids like Jessica and Tommy. Will you take the challenge of the Apostle Paul to let the love of Christ compel you?

Being capable of love and compelled by love—that is what will get us on the campus and keep us there.

TAKING ACTION

"Channel of Love" Strategy

As you meditate on 1 Timothy 1:5, ask the Lord to speak to you about your capacity to love. Then ask yourself:

1. What motives, besides a selfless love for students, cause me to want to minister on the campus?

_____

_____

_____

2. What are God's pure motives for me to go on the campus?

_____

_____

_____

3. In what area(s) do I need to unclog sin so that God's love for students will flow through me?

____pure heart

____good conscience

____sincere faith

According to the blanks you checked, answer the appropriate questions.

PURE HEART

In what ways is my heart not pure?

_____

_____

_____

What sins do I need to confess?

_____

_____

_____

In what ways am I not single-mindedly focused on Jesus Christ?

_____

_____

_____

GOOD CONSCIENCE

To whom do I need to go and ask forgiveness (Matthew 5:23-24)?

_____

_____

_____

Whom do I need to forgive so that I can rid myself of resentment and bitterness (Matthew 18:15)?

_____

_____

_____

_____ Check here when you have resolved the relational conflicts that keep God's love from flowing through you.

SINCERE FAITH

In what specific ways have you presented a deceptive, dishonest impression of your walk with Christ?

_____

_____

_____

Who is one person to whom you can confess your sin?

_____

_____

Now, as you contemplate 2 Corinthians 5:14, ask Christ to compel you to love kids who need Him.

4. In what ways do you need to shift your focus from the physical world to the realm of spiritual reality?

_____

_____

_____

5. Reflecting on your ministry, how would you respond to the statement: "My goals control my life more than my life controls my goals"?

_____

_____

_____

6. After identifying the frustrations you feel when kids fail to respond, what do you think God wants you to do with your frustrations?

_____

_____

_____

_____

_____

7. List the names of five non-Christian kids with whom you have strong relationships. Describe your relationship with each one in a sentence or two.

_____

_____

_____

_____

_____

_____

_____

_____

_____

_____

_____

_____

_____

_____

_____

NOTES

1. W. E. Vine, *The Expanded Vine's Expository Dictionary of New Testament Words*, Special Edition, ed. by John R. Kohlenberger III (Minneapolis, MN: Bethany House Publishers, 1984), 693.

THREE

BEND YOUR KNEES

"You mean prayer can really make a difference?"

It was 5:26 AM. Friday. Cold. Dark. Not a sound except my breathing. I sat in my car facing the school. Stay awake! Keep warm! To amuse myself I blew smoke rings with my breath, fogging my windshield. After my third game of tic-tac-toe on my windshield (the rubber match), a pair of headlights rounded the corner of the school and headed toward my car. As it pulled closer, I said to myself, "I've never seen headlights float in midair." The darkness and my foggy windshield gave the car the appearance of being suspended in space. Then out stepped my friend John, the other youth leader on campus. I felt a surge of energy. Now I could begin my most important appointment of the week. For one year we had come to the school to walk around it and to pray for God to move on the campus. Out of frustration and failure we had learned that just going to the campus wasn't getting the job done, no matter how much time we spent, how well we planned our attack, or how many leaders helped us. We had come to pray because we had learned that success on that campus was only a bent knee away!

John Bunyan, author of *Pilgrim's Progress* and a powerful man of prayer, said, "You can do more than pray after you've prayed, but you cannot do more than pray until you have prayed."

A person who prays has learned that success in any endeavor comes only from having the hand of God upon it. That's why the psalmist wrote: "Unless the Lord builds the house, its builders labor in vain" (Psalm 127:1). The Apostle Paul pressed the same point this way: "I planted the seed, Apollos watered it; but God, made it grow. So neither he who plants nor he who waters is anything, but only God, who makes things grow" (1 Corinthians 3:6-7).

"You can do more than pray after you've prayed,
but you cannot do more than pray until you have prayed."
John Bunyan

For God to work on a campus, youth workers must commit to sacrificial prayer. J. Edwin Orr calls it "extraordinary prayer." In his message "The Role of Prayer in Spiritual Awakening" Orr explains:

> What do we mean by extraordinary prayer? We share in ordinary prayer in regular worship services, before meals and the like. But when people are found getting up at six in the morning to pray, or having a half night of prayer until midnight, or giving up their lunch time to pray at a noonday prayer meeting, that is extraordinary prayer.[2]

In the context of those comments, Dr. Orr paints a picture of the youth culture in the wake of the American Revolution. He quotes the observations of Lyman Beecher, who described a typical campus in 1795:

> College was in a most ungodly state. The college church was almost extinct. Most of the students were skeptical and rowdies were plenty. Wine and liquors were kept in many rooms; intemperance, profanity, gambling and licentiousness were common — most of the class before me were infidels and called each other Voltaire, Rousseau, - - - etc.?

Dr. Orr then goes on to explain how widespread this problem was:

> What was true at Yale in New Haven was true at Princeton in New Jersey, there being in one year no more than two students who professed religion, only five or six who scrupled the use of profane language in common conversation—and in the "filthy speech" movement the profanity sometimes was of a very shocking kind. So far as religion was concerned, the colleges were the seed-beds of infidelity. The University of Pennsylvania, Transylvania College, Columbia College in South Carolina, and others had influential "free-thinkers" on their faculties. An anti-Church play was featured at Dartmouth. At Yale and Princeton, as at William and Mary, the student bodies were overwhelmingly skeptical, if not infidel. At Bowdoin, as at Yale, the number of believers was counted on one hand. During the last decade of the eighteenth century, the typical Harvard student was atheist.

Students at Williams College conducted a mock celebration of Holy Communion. When the Dean at Princeton opened the chapel Bible to read, a pack of playing cards fell out, some radical having cut a rectangle out of each page to fit the pack. Christians were so unpopular that they met in secret and kept their minutes in code. The radical leader of deist students led a mob in burning the Bible of a Raritan Valley Presbyterian church. Students disrupted worship services with both profanity and sputum. They burned down buildings; and they forced the resignation of college presidents. Young Christians had their backs to the wall.[4]

We live in a very similar environment today, as we learned from chapter one. Safely we can say that a definite numbness, blind apathy, and even outright rebellion exist toward the things of God. If ever we needed prayer, we need it now. In light of that need, let's walk through the famous passage in 2 Chronicles 7:14 to get a fresh glimpse of the way to bend our knees for the younger generation:

If my people, who are called by my name, will humble themselves and pray and seek my face and turn from their wicked ways, then will I hear from heaven and will forgive their sin and will heal their land.

HUMBLY DEPEND ON GOD

After love, humility stands as the most important quality of a Christian leader. That's because humility recognizes the need for a person to be totally dependent on God for everything, no matter how big or small. The writer of Chronicles calls on people to "humble themselves." That humble attitude leads a person to pray.

Charles Spurgeon made this assessment: "Humility is to make a right estimate of one's self"[5]

**"Humility is to make a right estimate of one's self."
Charles Spurgeon**

A. W. Tozer explained that right estimate.

The meek man is not a human mouse inflicted with a sense of his own inferiority. Rather he may in his moral life be as bold as a lion and as strong as Samson; but he has stopped being fooled by himself. He has accepted God's estimate about his own life. He knows he is as weak and helpless as God declared him to be. But paradoxically he knows at the same time that he is in the sight of God more important than angels. In himself nothing, in God everything. That is his motto.[6]

And that is humility.

In 2 Corinthians 12:9, the Apostle Paul describes how humility works. "But [God] said to me, 'My grace is sufficient for you, for my power is made perfect in weakness.' Therefore I will boast all the more gladly boast about my weaknesses, so that Christ's power may rest on me." God works in the lives of people totally subjected to Him.

That reality dawned on me while talking to a friend who had an addiction to cocaine. He accepted Christ five years ago. For those five years he knew drugs were wrong. With all of his heart he wanted to live for Christ, but he had no strength to do so. He tried several different ways to quit. He promised God several times he would never do drugs anymore. But he failed time and time again. As we talked, he spoke with desperation.

> I want so badly to be free. I want so badly to be clean. I want to show God that I can do it, to prove to him that I do love Him. But I know I can't do it. I've come to realize that it is impossible for me to quit. I just want to give up.

Out of desperation he had placed himself in exactly the right position—total, humble dependence.

And that's exactly where God wants us. We must realize that God ultimately does the work. God does not need us, but we need Him. When we realize this, we will move quickly into His presence, fall on our faces, and pray with desperation.

Leonard Ravenhill, the well-known author and speaker on revival, explains the importance of desperate prayer:

> Now I say very often - - - that God doesn't answer prayer. He answers desperate prayer! Your prayer life denotes how much you depend on your own ability and how much you really believe in your heart when you sing, "Nothing in my hands I bring, simply to the cross I cling. . ." The more

self-confidence you have, the less you pray. The less self-confidence you have the more you have to pray.[7]

Are you desperate to pray? Do you still depend on your own strength and abilities to change the lives of students? Or are you desperately seeking God to do His work on the campus? A man who humbly depends on God prays desperately.

HEARTILY PRAY TO GOD

A humble attitude, then, will drive us to pray (2 Chronicles 7:14). The Hebrew word for *pray* means to intercede for, to stand in the gap on behalf of another person. This word has two emphases: (1) meeting with God, and (2) meeting with God on behalf of someone else. A person praying in this way carries a burden, a strong concern manifested by persistently meeting with the One who can do something to make a difference.

Only this "strong burden" in prayer will ensure our success in seeing lives change on the campus. If the Good News of Jesus Christ is going to impact the campus, it will happen because we are coming to the Lord consistently on the students' behalf.

Dr. Paul Yonggi Cho, the pastor of the largest church in the world, urges us to pray heartily.

> No people have ever given more for the preaching of the gospel than the people from the United States of America. No country has ever sacrificed its own to save others from the oppression of tyranny more than the American people. Why, then, is there not a nationwide revival? The answer is a lack of prayer.[8]

"Why, then, is there not a nationwide revival? The answer is a lack of prayer." Paul Cho

To illustrate that point, last year we were experiencing one of the driest times in our ministry in terms of people coming to know the Lord. In addition, we had seen many converts turn away from their faith. After several months, the Lord impressed on me the need to begin a prayer meeting each week to ask God to send His Spirit to that high school. (I don't know why I always pray last instead of first!) We did not change our normal agenda except to add intense, extraordinary prayer. Within a brief time, I could account for 18 decisions for Jesus Christ. Most significantly, 17 of those students have stayed strong in their faith over the long haul.

It's not too difficult to generate programs and even gather large numbers of kids. But the real measure of a ministry is how many come out the other end having experienced life change in Jesus Christ. Our goal: to produce life-changers for the kingdom of God. Our first major step to achieving that kind of life-changing success is only a bent knee away.

If you are looking for some practical ways to get started, try these ideas:

1.SET A TIME TO PRAY

Rearrange your schedule to find a block of time or several smaller blocks every week when you can pray for your students. Put it on your schedule and determine not to move it. Experience says that if you change the time, prayer will slide right out of your schedule. Try to make it early in the morning before most activity starts.

To solidify your commitment to do this, look at your schedule now and fill in the time and day to pray.

I commit to pray _____(day) at _____(time).

2. DETERMINE A LOCATION FOR PRAYER

Pray where the action is. I always go right to the front door of the school. Obviously you have to get there early in order not to get trampled by the kids. Determine where the best place to meet is, then commit to be there.

I commit to pray at_____ (location).

3. ASK OTHERS TO PRAY

Find two other people who have a heart for students to pray with you. It will work best if all of you have a concern for the same campus. Possibilities include someone on your Leadership Team or a youth leader at another church, preferably even someone from another denomination. Praying with someone else will keep you accountable. Something about a friend waiting in the dark by himself tends to motivate you to get out of bed.

Also, praying with two others fits beautifully into a "prayer triplets" strategy of mobilizing your students to pray. Three Christians get together to pray three times week, each one for three of their non-Christian friends. (We will discuss this strategy thoroughly later in the book.) Write down the names of the other two people with whom you will pray.

I will ask (1) _____ and (2)
_____ to pray with me.

4.   DO NOT COMPROMISE YOUR TIME TO PRAY

Many demands will compete for your time. Satan will try to derail you. Don't let him. Repeat the following line as a prayer of your commitment to intercede for your students.

Lord Jesus, with Your help, I will intercede for young people!

HOPEFULLY SEEK GOD'S FACE

Equipped with a humble attitude and a specific commitment to pray, the words of 2 Chronicles 7:14 instruct us about how to pray. God says to "seek his face." In the Greek, the word "seek" means to look earnestly with the intent of finding the object. It implies a non-wavering commitment to locate something. The "something" to be found, in this case, is God's face. The word "face" means God's presence, His personality. This changes the focus of our prayers. Instead of praying for Mike not to act like such a jerk, we should pray for the Presence, the Person of God to reveal Himself to Mike. Our prayers need to focus not on what God does, but on who He is.

Many times we get caught up in manipulative praying. We get a picture in our own minds of what needs to happen in a person's life. So we pray for those circumstances we believe ought to happen. We pray that Peter Party will stop going to parties. But maybe God has a different plan. Maybe God wants to use those parties to show Peter how empty he is.

I used to pray that the football team would lose. I figured that if the players were sad, they would be more open spiritually. But instead they became even more closed. They thought that if they had won they wouldn't be so empty. So this year I'm praying they will win. Then they won't have an excuse for being empty, unless their girlfriends dump them. Then I don't know what I'll pray for.

Think about your own life. When you came to Christ, was it because you grasped the unconditional love of God for the first time? Were you attracted to who Jesus is, His person? When I realized who God is for the first time, all the pieces of the puzzle began to fall into place. When we seek God's face and pray that He will reveal who He is to young people, then we will learn to pray God's heart for students. When God answers those prayers, we will see that our success in youth ministry is only a bent knee away!

You may find this procedure helpful as a practical approach to "seek God's face" when you meet to pray on behalf of your students.

1.   *Ask God to give you His heart and words for your prayer time.* Be quiet before the Lord. As you spend more time listening to God, you will get more of His advice and He will get less of yours. (5 minutes)

2.   *Confess to the Lord any sins that the Holy Spirit has shown you.* Ask God to make you and your fellow workers transparent and vulnerable with each other. (5 minutes)

3.   *Praise and thank the Lord for all He has done in your personal life, in the lives of the students, and on the campus.* (Don't forget to thank Him for getting you up!) (5 minutes)

4.   *Share briefly anything God has brought to your attention this week regarding the students; any word on reaching out to kids; any insight from Scripture; any fruit.* (5 minutes)

5.   *Focus on spiritual awakening among the Christians on the campus.* Pray for Christian students by name, asking God to awaken them spiritually. Envision Christians interceding for their friends, serving the Lord Jesus Christ, and witnessing boldly. (10 minutes)

6.   *Concentrate on praying for lost students.* Pray for them by name. Pray that a movement of God's Spirit will sweep across the campus drawing young people to Christ. (10 minutes)

7. *Wait on the Lord for insight.* God will only bless what He initiates; therefore, wait before Him to see what He tells you to do as a result of your prayers. Do the next thing God tells you to do. (10 minutes)

Wait on the Lord for insight.
God will only bless what He initiates.

HONESTLY TURN FROM SIN

With a humble attitude, a specific commitment to pray, and a direction on how to pray, now we learn what to pray for. The clue is found in 2 Chronicles 7:14. The passage tells us to "turn away from" and "turn to." We turn away from anything that hinders God's active presence in our lives, and we turn to Christ and embrace Him fully. To "turn from [your] wicked ways" implies not only a mental and spiritual confession but also an actual physical movement. Prayer leads to action!

The personal form of the words *turn from your wicked ways* challenges us to deal with the sin in our personal lives. No doubt as you continue to meet with God on behalf of students and listen for His voice, He will show you what action to take regarding any sin in your own life. He will reveal current sin that hinders your walk with Christ and your ministry. He will do that because He wants you to become more of a pure prayer instrument in His hands. There's no question that a man or woman who prays extraordinary prayers will be called upon to live an extraordinary life. Decide now to do all God asks of you.

A man or woman who prays extraordinary
prayers will be called upon to live an extraordinary life.

To "turn from your wicked ways" applies to corporate sin as well. When you pray, ask God to show you the sins present in the school. Write them down. Your group can repent and confess on behalf of the school. Then ask Him to let you see the strongholds that have resulted from those sins (2 Corinthians 10:4-5). What "root is producing the fruit"? What stronghold is producing the outward manifestations of sin? Identify those strongholds and acknowledge them to the Lord. Then ask God to show you the powers and authorities in the spiritual realm. What "principalities and powers" are operating over the school? (See Ephesians 6:11-12). When you pray that way, you will see incredible victory in the spiritual battle for your school. Your action as an intercessor moves the school and the individuals in it to "turn from their wicked ways."

This kind of intercession can happen only when a person is significantly involved with the people for whom he prays. In the biography *Rees Howell: Intercessor*, Norman Grubb describes through the life of this man of prayer how this personal involvement works. "He [the intercessor] pleads effectively because he gives his life for those he pleads for."[9] Grubb goes on to say: "That is the law of intercession in every area of life, that only so far as we have been tested and proved willing to do a thing ourselves, can we intercede for others."[10] Unless we willingly involve ourselves in the concerns of a person's life, or those of the school, we cannot effectively intercede for anyone. Getting involved gives us the inside track to know how to pray properly.

For two years God asked me to sweep gym floors for a coach and thirteen wrestlers who couldn't have cared less about me. I spent two years giving them water and cleaning up their sweat. For two years I got the "what-in-the-world-are-you-doing-here" stare. But for two years I interceded for that school. Those two years opened wide the doors of that school to my ministry. I had to pay the intercessor's price for success.

You may ask questions like: "Does this really work? If I bend my knees the way the God of 2 Chronicles tells me to, will I be a success? Will the school experience a real movement of God's Spirit?" The last phrase in 2 Chronicles 7:14 promises that once we have humbled ourselves and prayed, sought God's face, and turned from our wicked ways, then He "will hear from heaven and will forgive [our] sins and will heal [our] land."

Although God will never be manipulated by man, He does want to hear, forgive, and heal. Dr. G. Campbell Morgan provides us with an eternal perspective: "We cannot organize revival, but we can set our sails to catch the wind from heaven when God chooses to blow upon His people once again."[11] Although prayer does not guarantee that you will successfully reach every student on your campus for Christ, Scripture and history indicate that a spiritual awakening has never come without bent knees.

"We cannot organize revival, but we can set our sails to catch the wind from heaven when God chooses to blow upon His people once again." G. Campbell Morgan

At the beginning of the chapter, we quoted J. Edwin Orr describing the youth culture after the American Revolution. We identified it as being very similar to our youth culture today. Let's look at what God did. Dr. Orr describes here one of many dynamic examples of the results of extraordinary prayer.

At Harvard, Bowdoin, Brown, Dartmouth, Middlebury, Williams, and Andover, new societies were formed. To resist the ungodly influences that prevailed, they committed themselves to mutual watchfulness, ardent prayers, frequent fellowship, mutual counsel and friendly reproof. In most cases, they were tiny societies. For example, three students at Brown University formed a "college praying society," which met weekly in a private room, "for fear of disturbance from the unpenitent." About the same time—11th December 1802—three juniors and four sophomores formed themselves into the Harvard Saturday Evening Religious Society. It also was a secret society in its early years. [12]

The results were dramatic!

The evangelistic impact of the days of prayer on campus was noteworthy. Amherst, Dartmouth, Princeton, Williams and Yale, to name a few, reported the conversion to God of a third to a half of their total student bodies.[13]

As we move about in our twenty-first century world, S. D. Gordon challenges us to practice that same kind of prayerful success.

The great people of the earth today are the people who pray. I do not mean those who talk about prayer; nor those who say they believe in prayer; but I mean those people who take time and pray. These are the people today who are doing the most for God: in winning souls; in solving problems; in awakening churches; in keeping the old earth sweet awhile longer.[14]

For you, success is only a bent knee away!

TAKING ACTION

Campus Prayer Strategy

Design your strategy of prayer for your campus or campuses by completing these exercises.

1. Record the circumstances that have brought you to the place of desperate prayer.

_____

_____

_____

2. Describe the barriers in front of you that keep you from humble dependence on God.

_____

_____

_____

_____

3. Write a short description of what you believe God would like to do on the campuses in your city.

_____

_____

_____

_____

4. Make some decisions about having an extraordinary time of prayer for the campus: Who will pray with you?

_____

Where will you meet?

_____

At what time will you meet?

_____

How long will each meeting last?

_____

5. Develop the prayer plan you will use for your first meeting, using the suggestions found on page 42.

_____

_____

_____

_____

_____

6. Make a preliminary assessment of what you see as the spiritual condition of the campus.

Sins:

_____

_____

Strongholds:

_____

_____

Spiritual powers:

_____

_____

7. Like the spiritual awakening in the late 1700s, revival is coming to the young people in America. What do you think it will look like? What do you need to do to prepare for it?

_____

_____

_____

_____

_____

_____

NOTES

1. John Bunyan, "Reflections on Prayer," in Tabletalk (Ligonier Ministries) vol. 11, no. 12. (Feb. 1987), 5.

2. J. Edwin Orr, The Role of Prayer in Spiritual Awakening (New York Oxford, 1976), 8.

3. J. Edwin Orr, Campus Aflame (Glendale, Calif.: Regal Books, 1971), 19.

4. Ibid.

5. Quotation from Charles Spurgeon found in George Sweeting, ed., Great Quotes and illustrations (Waco, Tex.: Word Books, 1985), 146.

6. Quotation from A. W. Tozer found in Sweeting, ed., Great Quotes And illustrations;145-146.

7. Leonard Ravenhill, "Prayer" (Last Days Ministries tract).

8. Dr. Paul Yonggi Cho, "America, It's Time to Pray," The Forerunner (April 1984), 12.

9. Norman Grubb, Rees Howell. Intercessor (Fort Washington, Pa.: Christian Literature Crusade, 1984), 87.

10. Ibid., 98.

11. Stephen Olford, Lord Open the Heavens (Wheaton, IlL: Harold Shaw, 1980), 92.

12. Orr, Campus Aflame, 25.

13. Ibid., 27.

14. S. D. Gordon, Quiet Talks on Prayer (Westwood, NJ.: Fleming H. Revell, 1967), 11.

PART TWO

MOVE FROM THE OUTSIDE TO THE INSIDE

FOUR
BUILD THE BRIDGE

"Wow, schools sure have changed since..."

As I walked onto the campus, one student I knew ran up and began to tell me about a man who had shown up on the campus with a box of Bibles, handing them out at the front door to anyone who would take one. This had created quite a stir. I went over to watch. The principal told the man he would have to leave. His response: "These students have a right to the Word of God." He refused to move. The principal called security, who quickly escorted the man off the campus.

Getting on a campus (and staying on) involves much more than showing up with a box of Bibles and demanding your rights. In fact, it calls for just the opposite.

All over the country people tell me that getting on their school campus is impossible. I know that some campuses are more closed than others. But even if the administration has a totally closed mind to religious people coming on campus, you can have an effective campus ministry. If you carefully follow biblical principles, *you can get on any campus in the United States—and stay on.* How can you do it?

KNOW THE SCHOOL

To get on campus and stay on, you start by knowing the school situation. An experience I had while playing basketball with Athletes in Action helps to illustrate the value of this principle. Our team set up two games with the Yugoslavian national team soon after they had won the 1980 Olympics. We had only two months to prepare. The next two months we ate, slept, and drank Yugoslavian basketball. Beginning at 9:00 AM each day, the scrubs (that included me) ran the Yugoslavian offense. For four hours each afternoon we watched videos of the Yugoslavian team playing everyone else in the world. We watched and rewatched, rewinding every play until we knew their strategy exactly.

You can get on any campus in the United States—and stay on.

By the end of those two months we knew every play they had run since they had become a team! We knew every player's strengths and weaknesses and how they acted in any given situation. We knew their favorite Chinese restaurant and their favorite video games. When we played, we won both games. I even came off the bench and made a jump shot. We won because we knew everything about that team. As difficult and time-consuming as the preparation was, when the time came to play, we were ready! The point: the more you prepare by knowing the school, the greater the possibility of "winning" with a successful ministry on that campus.

To prepare ourselves for ministry on the campus, let's see what the Apostle Paul did in Athens (Acts 17:16-34). The situation we face in the public school system parallels Paul's situation.

Paul had arrived only recently in Athens, where he was waiting for Timothy and Silas to come at any moment from Berea. While he waited, he looked around. What he saw burdened him. Acts 17:16 tells us that "he was greatly distressed to see that the city was full of idols." That same distress will grip us when we look around on the public school campus. So what did Paul do?

> He then stood up in the meeting of the Areopagus and said: "Men of Athens! I see that in every way you are very religious. For as I walked around and looked carefully at your objects of worship, I even found an altar with this inscription: TO THE UNKNOWN GOD. Now what you worship as something unknown I am going to proclaim to you" (Acts 17:22-23).

At one time the Areopagus served as an authoritative council that ruled the Greek city-state. But by the time of Paul's visit it had lost most of its authority to make decisions and instruct the people. Doesn't that have a strong resemblance to the American public school system and your local school?

From Paul's actions at the Areopagus, we can discover some important principles regarding how to open the right door to get on the campus.

DETAIL THE SCHOOL

The Apostle Paul made a detailed observation of his situation. Rather than barreling in, he took the time to understand the environment. He took a "walking tour" of Athens. In Acts 17:22-23 he says, "I see that in every way you are very religious. For as I walked around..." The Greek word translated "see" in this verse means "to view attentively in order to find out with certainty." "To walk around" speaks of the continuous action of passing through, not just a one-time look. When a person "walked around," he did so with the intent of getting a thorough, detailed perspective on the environment.

Philosophical and religious fervor dominated Athens. Motivated by the discovery of new religions and philosophies, people would sit for hours, talking, making up new philosophies. Paul observed that environment as he walked around.

In the same way, you can walk around and observe your school. That puts you in a position to know your school. Put yourself in situations that give you exposure to the school. Get a sense of the heart of that school, its basic personality. Each school has a different personality. How can you know the personality of your school?

Put yourself in situations that give you exposure to the school.

ATTEND SCHOOL EVENTS

Practically all school events are open to the public. Several steps will help you expedite the process of getting in to these events.

STEP 1: DECIDE WHAT EVENTS TO ATTEND

Most school events fall in two categories: athletic and nonathletic. Athletic events include football, basketball, cheerleading, cross-country, wrestling, swimming, track, tennis, gymnastics, soccer, golf, and baseball. They may even have synchronized swimming, but I wouldn't hold my breath (pun intended). Nonathletic events consist of dramas, musicals, band, drill team, chorus, beauty pageants, debate and forensic competition, homecoming parades, and bonfires.

Many other clubs have competitions also. Use the list above to spur your thinking so you can decide what events interest you.

STEP 2: OBTAIN THE EVENTS SCHEDULE

For a comprehensive events schedule, call the school office. Ask if you can get the schedules of all of the school's events. If an event of interest to you is not included, ask for the schedule of that team, organization, or club. You may need to talk to the person in charge of that particular school organization, but usually the school office can furnish you with a comprehensive schedule for the coming months.

If a school official asks you why you want a schedule, tell the truth. Say that you are a scout with Duke University. Just kidding! Say that you live in the community and would like to support the school.

STEP 3: FILL IN YOUR CALENDAR

After you have the schedules in hand, put as many events as possible on your calendar for the next two months. In two months, you can get to know a school well if you focus on attending events. Attend at least one event a week. And while you are at it, take someone with you who helps with the youth ministry.

STEP 4: OBSERVE THE SCHOOL

As a part of your "walking tour" of the school, go to an event that the majority of the school population will attend, such as a football game. At a football game you will find in one place the football team, the band, the cheerleaders, the drill team, a huge boosters club (parents), most of the faculty, and a few referees.

When you go to the events, arrive early and leave late. Arriving early may give you an opportunity to talk to some of the participants in the event (the team, the cast, etc.). Once the event begins, step back, look, and listen. Take in all you can. Ask yourself these questions:

- What in the world am I doing here? (Just kidding.)
- What different groups are represented here?
- What motivates these kids?
- What do they wear?
- What is cool to them?

- What is not cool? (Probably what you are wearing!)
- Do the black, white, Hispanic, and Asian kids sit together?
- Are kids drunk?
- Do kids sit by themselves?
- Do kids pay attention?
- Do they cut down each other?
- What characterizes the largest group?
- What attitudes are detectable?
- What is the faculty like?
- What motivates the faculty?
- Are many parents in attendance?
- Do moms and dads sit together?
- How do people respond when someone messes up?
- Was a public or team prayer offered before the event?

There are many other questions you can ask, but if you can answer these questions in particular you will get a pretty good feel for the school.

STEP 5: MAKE A JOURNAL OF WHAT YOU SEE

Write down your impressions as soon as you see some worth noting. Jot down the names of the people you met and what you learned about them. Review and add to this list frequently. I put this information on my handheld computer. At the first opportunity I write down the names and descriptions of the people I met as well as observations about the school. After keeping a journal of several events you can look back over your notes and begin to get an overall feel for the school.

In two months, you can get to know a school well if you focus on attending events.

STUDY THE SCHOOL YEARBOOK

To know a school quickly and easily, study the school yearbook. To obtain a copy, call the school office to see if they have extra yearbooks from last year. If they do, ask if you can buy one. Since a yearbook depreciates quickly, especially if someone else's name has been written in it, they will usually sell you the yearbook for a very reasonable price. If no yearbooks are available, ask one of your students if you can borrow a copy. (Also, you can find out what this kid is up to by reading what people wrote about him in the yearbook!)

Once you get a yearbook, look through it, asking yourself the same questions that you did at the events. Look for the people or events that take up most of the pages. Since students prepare the yearbook, you can be sure they will emphasize who or what they consider most important. The yearbook will serve as a handy reference book about the school.

SUBSCRIBE TO THE SCHOOL NEWSPAPER

Most schools have a newspaper that students fill with their personal opinions about hot school issues. They usually like to push the limits of their "freedom of the press" with the administration. From the newspaper, you can learn what students think about a wide range of issues—from abortion to school lunches to the best places to hang out. To get a copy, call the school office. Find out how frequently the paper comes out and how you can obtain copies.

INTERVIEW STUDENTS

Hopefully, you already know some students at the school. Set up appointments with four to eight of these students to ask them questions about the school. The following questions will give you ideas for your interviews.

- What is your favorite aspect of school (besides the final bell)?
- What is your least favorite part of school life (besides cafeteria "mystery meat")?
- What's "in"? What's not "in"?
- What different groups make up the student body of your school?
- Where do most of the students hang out?
- What do they do?
- Who are the popular students? Who makes up the "in" group?
- Who are the unpopular students?
- What is your principal like?

- What are your teachers like?
- Who are the popular teachers?
- Who are the unpopular teachers?
- How do teachers exercise discipline?
- Who are the Christian teachers?
- What Christian groups meet on campus?
- What activities do you participate in?

INTERVIEW TEACHERS

Teachers will give you great insights into the students. In addition, they will provide an inside look at the administration, especially the principal's perspective. Set up interviews with two or three teachers and ask them the following questions:

- What is the most positive aspect about teaching here?
- Do you like teaching at this particular school?
- What significant problems do the teachers face?
- What do teachers like doing least at the school?
- What major problems do the students face?
- What is your principal like?
- Do you think he or she would object to me coming on the campus? Why or why not?
- What Christian groups are active on this campus (for example, teachers' prayer groups, moms' prayer groups, student Bible studies or clubs, Christian organizations)?
- Where do volunteers fit in (for example, people to answer the phone, ushers at ball games, sponsors, coaches, etc.)?
- What are the greatest needs of the school?

Teachers can become your greatest allies! Remember, effective campus ministry will involve teachers as well as students.

VISIT THE HANGOUTS

Although this idea is the scariest of these suggestions, it can give you mega-insights into what goes on in students' lives. You will see a different side of kids when they meet at a hangout. That doesn't mean you will see who they are, because they will still put on masks to impress their friends. But when they hang out, you can see them interact with one another beyond the boundaries of authority. You will observe their fears, insecurities, and values.

The big question you probably want answered now is "How in the world do I go where these kids hang out and not look like a narcotics officer?" Be honest! Haven't you always wanted to be an undercover youth leader? If not, maybe these guidelines will help.

1. *Don't go places where you are not wanted.* For example, you don't want to wander into a party just for kids. You probably couldn't get in anyway, but even if you did, the students would not welcome you.

2. *Do go to public places.* Fast-food restaurants, game rooms, malls, parking lots, and other places in your town where students hang out provide ideal places to observe students.

3. *Go to the weekend hangouts after football games.* The big hangout for my school is the Burger King parking lot. It serves as the hub of information. If one student needs to meet another one, they meet at Burger King.

I go to the local Burger King and order a Whopper, fries, and a Coke (with free refills). Then I sit and observe the students. Anyone can eat at Burger King and not appear to be weird. (Or is it that everyone else is weird already, so you fit right in?)

Once you know where the students hang out, stick to that place. Act as inconspicuously as a fly on the wall and observe. By the time you finish this two-month process, you will have received an education in youth ministry for free—except for the Whoppers, fries and Cokes!

DEFINE THEIR BASIC MOTIVATIONS

Once you have observed the school, organize the information you collected.

Remember the Apostle Paul in Athens (Acts 17:16)? We left him there several pages ago. As a result of his observations of the people in Athens, he could define their basic motivations. He told the assembled philosophers: "For as I walked around and looked carefully at your objects of worship..." (Acts 17:23). To "look careful-ly" means to look with interest and purpose; intense focus. "Object of worship" expresses that which is honored religiously. *Webster's* defines it as any object that is seriously pursued. Paul found their object of worship at an altar with this inscrip-tion: TO AN UNKNOWN GOD (v. 23).

Everyone has a god. We can define a "god" as anything that controls our lives, consumes our minds, or has a very high value to us. In effect, Paul tells them: you have an intense focus on something that you are seriously pursuing and that you put high value on, but you don't know what it is. It's amazing how much that sounds just like today's teenage culture! What "gods" control your kids' lives? Their campus?

Each school will have a few basic motivations that take precedence. What does the school value highly? Academics? Drugs? Parties? Athletics? In what sports do they excel? What activities dominate the school? In what areas have they succeeded? What is the school known for? In what do they take pride? As you discover these you will know the basic motivations of the school.

As you follow through with observing the school you will have a good under-standing of what it is like. Put all of this information in a orderly form on the "School Survey" at the end of this chapter.

SERVE A NEED

To get on the campus, find a need that the school does not have the manpower to fill, but that still needs to be done. When you know the school, you will know what needs exist. Notice that Paul didn't burst into the Areopagus passing out copies of the Equal Philosophy Act, telling these people they were going to hell for believing in these fake gods. No! Paul knew that truth shared with closed ears doesn't receive a hearing. Cleverly, he had to find a way to get these "philosophy prima donnas" to listen to him. He looked for an opening.

While Paul walked around Athens, he looked carefully at their objects of worship. He hunted for an opening, a need that he could meet, something to get him on the inside. Then he saw that they had an altar TO AN UNKNOWN GOD (Acts 7:23). Paul knew that Athenians liked philosophies and religions and that he could present the gospel by way of this topic. To get on a campus you have to exercise wisdom. Yes, we do have the truth that transforms lives. And, yes, we do have the solution to hopelessness, immorality, and a host of educational problems that schools face today. And, yes, it's a bummer that most administrations fight tooth and nail to keep the church out of the schools. And, no, it's not fair that humanistic philosophies have easy access to the campuses.

To get on a campus you have to exercise wisdom.

Be that as it may, our highest priority is still to give these students hope in Christ. To do that, we must lay aside our so-called rights for the sake of these students. It won't do any good to demand our rights to come on campus if that alienates us from the faculty and administration. That only removes us from the campus, away from the hurting students. We must lay down our rights. Let the lawyers fight those battles.

Our goal is to infiltrate the campus with Jesus-focused leaders who can move among the lives of hurting students. We want to position ourselves to develop relationships that will allow us to introduce Christ. We can do that when we sensitively discern a need, then serve that need rather than fighting for our rights.

To illustrate, one of my church youth leaders observed parents lugging heavy band equipment to and from football games. Every game, the same two guys carried the equipment. This leader volunteered to help them carry the equipment every week. Their response: "Get out of here. We like having hernia operations." Not really. They were grateful for the help. After a while the band director invited the leader to come to all the practices and school functions.

LOOK FOR WAYS TO MEET THE NEED

EVALUATE YOUR STRENGTHS

Think back. Once upon a time, before CDs, or for some, cassette players, or for others, eight-track players (look it up in the dictionary), you were in middle school and high school. Try to remember what you liked to do. What would you enjoy doing now? You don't have to excel at it, only make yourself available. If you need to, get the yearbook out again and flip through the section on clubs and other activities. That will stir your thinking. Write down five activities where you believe you can help. Remember your major role on the campus is serving, not impressing people with your abilities. As the saying goes: "They couldn't care less how much you know, until they know how much you care."

PRIORITIZE YOUR LIST OF NEEDS

Number the top five needs in order of priority. As you prioritize, think about the list in three ways: your strengths, school needs, contacts you have currently.

DETERMINE YOUR AVAILABILITY

Decide the times in your weekly schedule that you can commit. Can you help at school every day, every other day, or once a week? Can you attend practice or only the event? What time can you arrive, and when do you have to leave? Commit yourself only to what you know you can do! What will you commit to?

CONTACT THE APPROPRIATE PERSON

God has a place for you to serve. He will open the door, but you need to knock on it. Take the following steps to open the door:

- Find out who is in charge of the group you will serve.
- Make an appointment to see that person.
- Tell that person you have some time available to serve the school.
- Emphasize serving.
- If that person says no, go to the next contact person.
- Keep pressing on until you find an opening.

If you follow the suggestions in this chapter carefully, you will gain a specific knowledge of the campus and will have a specific reason to go on campus. By doing this first, you will already have an "in" at the school. Because you are not coming in cold, the principal is more likely to receive you. In the next chapter we have mapped out a way to help you gain the trust of the principal.

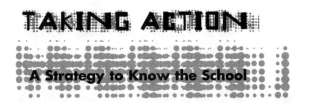

TAKING ACTION

A Strategy to Know the School

The action points for this chapter will take a considerable amount of research and time. It will take you more than a week and probably up to two months if you do it by yourself. SO, DO THIS AS A GROUP PROJECT WITH YOUR LEADERSHIP TEAM. Divide up responsibilities to speed up the process and to expand your perspective. This process entails three distinct projects. Each one must be completed before the other one can begin. Review the instructions in the chapter if needed.

1 CHECK OUT THE SCHOOL

Attend School Events

Step 1. *Obtain the schedules for the various activities.*

___Check here after calling the school office to get the schedule of events.

Step 2. *Fill in your calendar.*

___Check here when you have written the schedules of your top three activities on your calendar.

Step 3. *Decide the top three events you find most interesting.*

_____

_____

Step 4. *Observe the school.*

___Check here when you attend your first event.

Step 5. *Make a journal of what you see.*

___Check here when you have set up your journal.

___Check here after you have written your first journal entry.

STUDY THE SCHOOL YEARBOOK

___Check here when you have obtained a copy of the yearbook. Report the results of your study of the yearbook:

_____

_____

_____

_____

_____

_____

_____

_____

_____

SUBSCRIBE TO THE SCHOOL NEWSPAPER

___Check here when you have obtained a copy of the school newspaper. Report the results of your study of the school paper:

_____

_____

_____

_____

_____

_____

_____

_____

_____

_____

INTERVIEW STUDENTS

Write the names of two students you will interview.

_____

_____

Using the list of questions on pages 56-57, report your major conclusions about the school from talking to these students.

_____

_____

_____

_____

_____

_____

_____

_____

INTERVIEW TEACHERS

Write the names of two teachers you will interview.

_____

_____

Using the list of questions on page 57, report your major conclusions about the school from talking to these teachers.

_____

_____

_____

_____

_____

_____

_____

_____

_____

VISIT THE HANGOUTS

___Check here when you have gone to one hangout. Note your observations from that experience:

_____

_____

_____

_____

When you (and/or your group) have completed the projects in this section, go on to the next section.

2. DEFINE THEIR BASIC MOTIVATIONS

Now you want to put in order all of the input you collected during the previous step. To do that, complete the following School Survey.

SCHOOL SURVEY

School:

Address:

Phone:

Website:

Principal:

Contacts:

Teachers   Subjects and Activities

_____

_____

_____

_____

Students   Activities

_____

_____

_____

_____

Others   Relationship to school

_____

_____

_____

_____

(Put an asterisk by the names of the people with whom you have the best relationship.)

GROUPS

Identify the basic groups you have discovered on the campus (for instance, athletes, party animals, intellectuals, etc.)

_____

_____

_____

_____

_____

Which group appears to influence the campus the most?

_____

ISSUES

What are the major issues on the campus? (winning the football championship, abortion, busing, black/white relationships, death, etc.)

_____

_____

_____

_____

What main problems do students face? (Examples: drugs, family problems, sex, abuse, depression, etc.)

_____

_____

_____

_____

SOCIOECONOMIC FACTS

In what kinds of homes do the students live? (apartments, townhouses, middle-income houses, luxury homes)

_____

_____

Is your area urban or suburban?

_____

What is the economic status of this area?

_____

_____

What percentage of students would you estimate come from broken homes?

_____

_____

What percentage of the students are black?_____ white? _____ Hispanic? _____ Asian? _____ other? _____

SCHOOL HISTORY

How old is the school?

_____

What is the school's history?

_____

_____

_____

_____

What changes have taken place at the school during the last five years?

_____

_____

_____

How long has the current principal been at the school?

_____

How many principals have held that job in the last five years?

_____

In what community activities is the school involved?

_____

_____

_____

RELIGION

Is the administration open to religious groups having equal access with other organizations and clubs?

_____

Who spoke at graduation and baccalaureate services the last two years?

_____

What churches, Christian organizations, or other religions express interest in the campus?

_____

_____

What churches or Christian organizations do the students attend most frequently?

_____

_____

Who are the leaders of each of these groups?

_____

_____

Is there anything else unique to this school that would be helpful to know in ministering to this campus?

_____

_____

_____

In what areas of the school are volunteers needed?

_____

_____

_____

Once this section is completed, go on to the next section.

3 SERVE A NEED

FOLLOW THESE STEPS TO DISCERN A NEED

1. *List the needs.* List all the needs expressed by the people you have interviewed.

_____

_____

_____

_____

_____

_____

_____

_____

_____

Remember, there is no better way to show the love of Christ than to serve. Sweep the gym floor. Wash wrestling mats. Chaperone dances or other school activities. No job is too small or too menial, especially if it opens the door to students.

2. *Look for Ways to Meet The Needs.* Write down five specific activities where you believe you can help.

_____

_____

_____

_____

Number these activities in order of priority, then circle your highest priority.

3. Lock in your schedule. Determine how much time you can give to meeting this need, and at what time you can do it.

How much time can I give?

_____

When can I give this time?

_____

Who is the person to contact?

_____

Record that person's response here:

_____

_____

_____

FIVE

CROSS THE BRIDGE

"You mean I have to talk to the principal?"

John's heart continued to break for the students on the campus near his church. He wanted to reach those students for Christ. But the school was closed to any ministry coming on the campus. However, John was determined to get on that campus some way.

Then came the opportunity to substitute teach. Ideal. John would have access not only to the campus, but to hundreds of students for hours at a time.

When John taught he used his class time to give Christian answers to controversial subjects. As the students' interest increased, so did John's boldness. He enjoyed the opportunity.

John never bothered to meet with the principal. Truthfully, he felt a bit nervous about talking to him. The principal didn't even know John. When the principal heard about John's use of class time, he told John not to use the class to express his religious beliefs. Agitated, John argued with the principal. But the conversation ended when the principal said, "If I hear any more of this going on, then you won't teach here anymore."

John left infuriated. *How could this guy be a principal? He doesn't even care about giving these kids real-life answers.* John determined not to change anything he was doing. He felt that it was his duty to share Christ with these kids, even if he lost his job. He did. Quickly he retained an attorney who specialized in cases like this. The lawyer began to prosecute John's case of religious discrimination. I'm not sure where the case is now. But I am sure of one thing: Now that school has other substitute teachers who probably don't have the heart John has for those students. John is out. Even worse, because of John, other youth leaders are out too.

"But John had a right to express his faith, and those rights were violated," you might say. Were they? John has rights, but he stepped over the bounds of his authority when he argued with the principal and when he fought for his "rights" afterwards. Furthermore, John had not established the relationship with the principal that would have given him a basis for dealing with those issues positively. The world may operate that way, but God doesn't. If John had wanted to follow God's approach, he would have obeyed the school authorities.

RESPONDING PROPERLY TO SCHOOL AUTHORITIES

To have an effective campus ministry, we must understand the attitude of submission.

The Bible expresses this idea clearly in Romans 13:1-5:

> Everyone must submit himself to the governing authorities, for there is no authority except that which God has established. The authorities that exist have been established by God. Consequently, he who rebels against the authority is rebelling against what God has instituted, and those who do so will bring judgment on themselves. For rulers hold no terror for those who do right, but for those who do wrong. Do you want to be free from fear of the one in authority? Then do what is right and he will commend you. For he is God's servant to do you good. But if you do wrong, be afraid, for he does not bear the sword for nothing. He is God's servant, an agent of wrath to bring punishment on the wrongdoer. Therefore, it is necessary to submit to the authorities, not only because of possible punishment but also because of conscience.

To have an effective campus ministry, we must understand the attitude of submission.

Several points in these verses will help us to respond properly to school authorities.

1. *We have a command, not an option, to submit to authority.*

2. *God has established all authorities, whether they seem good or bad.* He wants us to submit to both.

3. *Not to submit to authority "brings judgment" that destroys our ministry instead of increasing it.*

4. *Submission opens doors and builds trust.* Remember that "rulers hold no terror for those who do right..."

5. *Submission releases us to minister freely on the campus because our "conscience" is clear toward authorities.*

The temptation to take matters into our own hands is great. But, after ministering on campus for many years, I have concluded that the road to students is easiest to travel when I have an attitude of submission to school authorities. It's not easy to stand by and watch what is taking place on the campus when. . .

. . . the school administration shows no interest in the spiritual aspect of kids' lives.

. . . the principal has become a pawn in the hands of the parents and the school board.

. . . the administration has a "make no waves" philosophy of school politics.

. . . the kids are going to hell in a handbasket, but the school turns its back on the solution.

The temptation to take matters into our own hands is great.

In spite of these issues, we must not take matters in our own hands. Nor must we believe the lie that "the administration has short-circuited the will of God, so all these kids will die without hearing the gospel." The truth is, NO ONE SHORT CIR-CUITS THE WILL OF GOD.

CULTIVATING A SUBMISSIVE APPROACH

You may be asking (I hope so), "How do I develop a submissive approach to the school authorities?" In Ephesians 6:5-8, the Apostle Paul sets forth three distinctives that characterize the serving Christian:

> Slaves, obey your earthly masters with respect and fear, and with sincerity of heart, just as you would obey Christ. Obey them not only to win their favor when their eye is on you, but like slaves of Christ, doing the will of God from your heart. Serve wholeheartedly, as if you were serving the Lord, not men, because you know that the Lord will reward everyone for whatever good he does, whether he is slave or free.

Let's look at how those distinctives will set you apart on the campus.

1. RESPECT

The Greek word for respect, *phobos*, means to treat with admiration or affection. To appreciate, even admire, the responsibilities of the school authorities gives us a positive perspective from the outset.

No doubt, high school principals have one of the most difficult jobs in America. They work 60-hour weeks. Hundreds of employees answer to them. They balance a budget that rivals those of many businesses. They carry the burden of students' problems and carry the nagging feeling that even their best efforts are inadequate for helping to solve those problems. They struggle with all the limitations placed on them by parents and the school board. The buck stops at their desk when anything goes wrong at the school. They report not only to their own supervisors, but also to hundreds of parents. In addition, principals carry the responsibility for the emotional well-being of their staff. They deal daily with one of the most precious commodities and controversial subjects in our society: our children and their education.

Thirty years ago the biggest offenses at school were talking, chewing gum, making noise, running in the halls, getting out of turn in line, wearing improper clothing, and not putting paper in the wastebasket. Today, the top offenses are rape, robbery, assault, burglary, arson, vandalism, extortion, drug and alcohol abuse, and murder. To protect the school, some principals have guard dogs, metal detectors, plainclothes police officers, and a security staff. Often they have to operate a day care center for students who have babies. The principal has to deal with very complex problems.

Most principals could easily get jobs paying more in the business world. But they choose to stay. Why? They care for young people. They may not share your beliefs, but in almost every case we can say, "They care."

If you want to increase your respect for the principal, look at him as a person with bills to pay and children to raise. The principal struggles with his own personal problems.

Ask God to give you a heart for the man or woman who bears responsibility for the campus. Grab hold of a genuine concern for the principal's concerns. Don't view him as a barrier you must get past to get on the campus. See the principal as God does: a person who, like everybody else, needs God's love.

If you want to increase your respect for the principal, look at him as a person with bills to pay and children to raise.

⟨. FEAR

Fear, in the context of Ephesians 6:5, actually means obedience. Wuest defines it as "solicitous zeal in the discharge of duty, anxious care not to come short."[1] If we were to apply this definition to the campus, we might describe it as "zealously taking care not to fall short in carrying out the wishes of the school administration."

For two years I worked very hard to develop a relationship with the boys' varsity basketball coach, all the time hoping he would invite me to help him coach. I felt this would open new doors to relationships that might not open up otherwise. Finally the day came when he asked me. *Ecstatic* described my feeling. At last I would have unlimited access to this group of students.

While sharing my excitement with a teacher friend at another school, he asked if I was aware of a rule that the only people allowed to coach were those currently teaching at the school. My friend felt that although everyone broke the rule, I had an obligation as a Christian to obey it. At first I didn't appreciate his opinion. But I knew he was right. I went back to the coach and asked about the rule. He said that he was aware of the rule, but it was his team and he could ask whomever he wanted to help out.

For a week I struggled, asking God if He knew what He was doing with this situation. I explained how many students, parents, and teachers I could reach by coaching. I told Him that "the end justifies the means." And I knew He was aware how much these kids needed me to help them win games. Besides, no one would care anyway.

After a week of these confusing conversations with the Lord, I told the coach that I couldn't help. He didn't understand. Most of the players didn't understand either. I wasn't even sure I understood. It seemed like my ministry was taking a giant step backward. But deep in my heart, I knew that my decision was right. I knew I had submitted properly.

You will run across these dilemmas yourself. But if you apply this distinctive of submission, you will have great personal freedom to minister on the campus.

3. SINCERITY

Sometimes I try to solve frustrating situations at school by letting the Lord know that a pagan stands in the way of His work. Obviously, this pagan isn't on the same wave-length as us (God, Jesus, the Holy Spirit, and me). Because this pagan isn't on God's side, I can bend the rules a little to get the situation worked out.

But in Ephesians 6:5-7, God spares me from wasting my time in this sea of rationalization. He speaks of "sincerity of heart" in phrases like:

"just as you would obey Christ."

"Obey them. . . when their eye is on you" (and we can infer "and even when it's not").

"Serve [them] wholeheartedly, as if you were serving the Lord."

You will encounter principals and school administrators who not only irritate you, but who are dead wrong. The only sincerely submissive response is to obey them and serve them as if they were Christ.

When you apply these three radical distinctives in submitting to the campus authorities, you will have set yourself apart not only in their eyes, but also in God's eyes. With these attitudes He will use you powerfully.

APPLYING SUBMISSION TO THE CAMPUS

How does submission work on the campus? For starters, when you apply an attitude of submission to the campus you will have a ministry there.

Let's walk through some steps on how to do that.

1. PRAY

Make prayer the essence of your preparation. The spiritual battle is at hand! Prepare to meet any opposition through prayer. Pray. . .
- that God would provide natural meetings with the school administration.
- that God would give you wisdom in these encounters.
- that the love of Jesus would flow through your life when you meet with the administration.
- that God would open the right door to the campus.
- that God would bring the school administrators to Christ.

2. MEET THE PRINCIPAL INFORMALLY

Certainly by now you have several contacts who know the principal personally. Arrange with one of your acquaintances to introduce you to the principal.

Usually the best time to initiate this informal contact is at an extracurricular event. In that setting the principal will have time to talk because he or she won't usually have major responsibilities. Ask your contact to introduce you as a person who works with young people, not as a youth pastor. You are not trying to hide anything, but you want to eliminate any presupposed stereotypes that would get your conversation off on the wrong foot. Never be deceptive. When the principal asks you where you work, respond honestly.

Speak positively about the school. Don't try to force conversation. Let him initiate it. Your primary goal is to make contact. Don't push the conversation beyond a comfortable limit.

When you talk to the principal, don't try to impress him. Be your friendly self. Let the Lord build the relationship. At the conclusion of the conversation, tell the principal how nice it was to meet him and that if you can ever help, not to hesitate to call. Let the principal know you can be reached through your mutual friend. This casual, informal contact will open the door to further relationship building in the days ahead.

3. WRITE THE PRINCIPAL A NOTE

The next day write a postcard thanking the principal for taking the time to meet you. For example:

> Dear Dr. Turner,
> It was a pleasure to meet you last night at the football game. I look forward to seeing you again soon. Please feel free to call me if I can serve you in any way.
>
> Sincerely,
> Tim Smith

Use a regular postcard instead of a church postcard unless you have already told the principal that you work for the church.

4. CALL FOR AN APPOINTMENT

Within a couple of weeks, call the principal. Follow this sample conversation.

> Hello, Dr. Turner, this is Tim Smith. I enjoyed meeting you at the game the other night. . . I am calling to see if I could meet with you for five minutes during the next week or two. I would like to talk to you about how I could serve the school.

If the principal asks what you mean by that, simply explain that you have a genuine concern for the students who live in your community. Say that you want to give to these students in some way by serving their school. When you talk to the principal, remember:

- Speak directly—don't beat around the bush.
- Express confidence, but not arrogance.
- Have your calendar ready so you can set the date quickly.

- Check your calendar beforehand to determine if some dates won't work for you.
- Accommodate his schedule as much as possible.
- Try to meet with him in person.
- Don't expect to be treated as an answer to prayer.
- After you set the appointment, thank him. Confirm the date and time of your meeting.

Tell the principal that you have a genuine concern for the students who live in your community.

5. MEET THE PRINCIPAL FORMALLY

In this appointment try to establish rapport with the principal. Share your concern for the school and your desire to help him. These guidelines will help to make this appointment successful.

- Before you enter the school, pray.
- Dress up. Don't wear old jeans and a T-shirt.
- Arrive ten minutes before the appointment and check in immediately with the secretary.
- Include these points in your conversation:
    - -Express appreciation for the time given you.
    - -Speak of your concern for young people.
    - -Share your respect for his authority and your desire to obey that authority.
    - -Tell of your availability to serve.

Your conversation should go something like this:

Hello, Dr. Turner. I want you to know how much I appreciate your time. I know that you are very busy. Dr. Turner, the reason I want to get together with you is that I have a deep concern for the students in my community and the problems they face today. I want to help them. It seems that one of the best ways I can help them is to help the school that helps them. I don't know everything that the school and its students need, but I do have some time available. I would like to volunteer that time to help in any way.

Let the principal take it from there. Don't keep talking. Honor the time commitment Also, anticipate questions. These questions are some of the ones I've been asked over the years:

"What do you do for a living?" Respond honestly. If you are a youth pastor, say so. Volunteer some details about the church. Assure him that you have no desire to proselytize students, but that you do have a genuine concern for their needs. If your occupation is a concern, assure him that you will not share your faith on campus.

"What interests and experiences have you had?" Tell him about your high school and college jobs. Let the principal know of your concern for students. Communicate clearly that you will do anything needed, from driving a bus to working in the refreshment stand.

"How much time are you willing to volunteer?" Study your schedule before the appointment so you can commit your available time on the spot.

"Why do you want to help the school?" Let the principal know you're aware that kids spend most of their waking hours on the campus. The public school serves as one of the most important influences in a student's life. Communicate, that by helping the school, you will help the students.

When the conversation is over, express thanks for the time you've been given. Leave your business card.

The principal may have no idea how you can help. That's fine. The purpose of this meeting is not to receive full access to the campus, but to begin opening doors by starting a relationship with the school's chief authority figure. Consider the meeting successful if you enhanced your relationship with the principal and developed his trust in you.

To continue building that relationship, observe the following "don'ts".
- Don't give the impression that you are an expert on students and schools.
- Don't insist that you have a right to come on campus.
- Don't make promises you can't keep. If you can volunteer only one day a week, then communicate that clearly.
- Don't share your opinions about such controversial subjects as abortion, church and state, prayer in schools, or anything else that might alienate the principal.

Keep the conversation centered on the school and how you can help it.

- Don't let the principal intimidate you. Although you should speak to this authority respectfully, you are also peers. If he tries to intimidate you, remember that you are an ambassador for Jesus Christ.
- Don't make demands. To represent Christ doesn't mean making demands. Rather, it means that you know God is in control. God will work through that principal to accomplish His will.

6. WRITE ANOTHER THANK-YOU NOTE

After meeting with the principal, write a note expressing your appreciation for his time. Here's an example:

Dear Dr. Turner,
Thank you for your time Tuesday morning. I know that you keep a very busy schedule. I appreciate you taking some of that time for me. Again, however I can serve you, I stand ready. My number is 706-555-8876.

Thank you,
Tim Smith

7. DECIDE ON AN AREA TO SERVE

By this time you have zeroed in on an area of need or interest. Now is the time to pursue helping in that area. Ask the teacher responsible if you can volunteer your time to help. Knowing the teacher beforehand will make a difference. To keep the teacher from feeling threatened, explain that you do not want to lead, but to serve.

8. FOLLOW UP WITH THE PRINCIPAL

After you have determined the place you will serve, make a follow-up appointment with the principal. The purpose of this appointment is to get his approval to serve on the campus. During the time before this appointment, attend at least two school activities where you will see the principal. Continue to let him know of your interest in the school and the students. During the appointment use the approach detailed in the following conversation, adjusting it to your area of service:

Hello Dr. Turner, I hope you are having a good day. Again, I appreciate your time. I have one specific issue to talk over with you. Coach Dawson has invited me to help with the wrestling team. He asked if I could videotape the practices. Seeing the video will help the wrestlers work on their moves. I want to get your approval before I make a commitment to Coach Dawson.

Wait for his response and pray (not out loud!).

PLAN A

If the principal says yes, then you are in; go to step #9. If he says no, then go to Plan B.

PLAN B

If the principal doesn't want you to serve in any way, don't let that discourage you. If you respond in the following manner, you will set a strong foundation for building the relationship.

1. *Write a thank-you note, even though the principal said no.* Express:
    –appreciation for the consideration you received.
    –appreciation for all he does for the students.
    –what a privilege it is to know him.
    –to please call if you can help in any way.

2. *Go to all of the extracurricular activities possible.* The principal or an assistant is required to attend. When you see him, continue a friendly tone of conversation. Look for serving opportunities outside the confines of the campus day (such as working at the concession stand at ball games or driving the bus for the band).

3. *Continue to pray for the principal and the school daily.* God will open the door as you serve.

9. WRITE ANOTHER THANK-YOU NOTE

After the appointment, regardless of whether the principal said yes or no or kicked you off the campus, make sure you express thanks for the time and effort he spends on behalf of the students. The following is an example of such a note:

Dear Dr. Turner,
Thanks again for the time you gave me. I appreciate all you do for the students at the school. Thank you for allowing me to come on the campus

and help with the wrestling team. I consider it a privilege to help.

Sincerely,

Tim Smith

706-555-8876

1 ■. CONTINUE TO BUILD THE RELATIONSHIP

Relate to the principal, not as a barrier or a stepping stone, but as a person. To help you continue to develop your relationship with the principal, keep in mind these points:

- Do what you say. If the principal asks you to do something, then do it responsibly.
- Periodically stop by the principal's office to speak to him.
- Any time you see the principal, stop and talk.
- Send notes of appreciation often. Let the principal know that you pray for his efforts to lead the school. Include in your notes congratulations on any school achievement (such as winning the county science fair or conference volleyball title).
- Ask permission for any privilege not expressly granted to you (coming on campus for a pep rally, for instance).
- Pray often for the principal and the school.

GETTING ON CAMPUS DURING SCHOOL HOURS

Many youth leaders try to get permission to come on the campus during lunch or to lead an early morning Bible study. Those times seem ideal for getting together with students. However, allow me to give you some compelling reasons for not spending time on campus during school hours.

1. It appears that you are serving your own agenda, not the school's agenda. You raise suspicion in the principal's eyes. Even though you have stated clearly that you want to serve the school, he gets the message that you have ulterior motives.

2. People who don't work for the school have no job description and no accountability. Principals have to deal with problems all day. The last thing they want is to have to deal with another "loose cannon."

3.   *Lunch and Bible studies are not the most productive times for campus ministry.* The best use of campus time involves helping students achieve their goals and initiating unhurried personal conversation. The after-school time slot allows the best opportunities for this kind of interaction. Conversely, lunchtime in the school cafeteria allows the least amount of time.

4.   *You get a label.* You will stand out at lunch. Non-Christian kids will label you as a youth pastor. To reach non-Christians you want to come across less as a youth pastor and more as a friend who cares.

In the past I have grown close to the principal at my school by following these steps. The relationship began in 1985 when he gave me permission to help sweep the basketball floor before practice. Two years ago he asked me to speak at the baccalaureate service for graduation. This invitation came not from the students (though that would have been nice too!), but from the principal. This year he told another teacher that he wishes that my type of campus involvement could happen on other campuses. In a county known for its closed schools I have the continuing privilege of going on the campus because I follow the Bible's principles of submission. You can too!

TAKING ACTION

A Strategy of Submission to School Authorities

Keeping in mind Romans 13:1-5 and Ephesians 6:5-9, describe God's view of how we should regard the authority of school officials.

_____

_____

_____

_____

_____

_____

Design your specific plan for building the relationship bridge with the principal at your school. Think and pray through each point, and write a detailed plan for each numbered item.

1. Pray.

_____

_____

_____

_____

2. Meet the principal informally.

_____

_____

_____

_____

3. Write the principal a thank-you note.

_____

_____

_____

_____

4. Call for an appointment.

_____

_____

5. Meet the principal formally.

6. Write another thank-you note.

7. Decide on an area to serve.

8. Follow up with the principal.

9. Write another thank-you note.

_____

_____

10. Continue to build the relationship. (Write down two things you will do to strengthen your relationship with the principal.)

_____

_____

_____

_____

NOTES

1. Kenneth Wuest, Word Studies in the Greek New Testament, vol. 1 (Grand Rapids: William B. Eerdmans Publishing Co., n.d.), 138.

SIX

KEEP THE BRIDGE OPEN

"Now that I'm in, what do I do?"

Watching the basketball team practice, I got excited about how I could help the team. As the coach worked with the players, I saw some definite room for improvement. I noticed that he had difficulty getting the players motivated—and that was my specialty. I had played basketball most of my life. I had worked in more basketball camps than I could remember. I knew the game. And I knew what that coach needed to do.

As I was picking him apart mentally, I also looked for an opening to talk to him. When he blew the whistle for a water break and walked toward me, I knew my chance had come. I jumped off the bleachers, extended my hand with my best used-car-dealer smile, and said "Hi, my name is Keith Naylor. The team looks pretty good." (That's not really what I thought, but how could I say, "Your team stinks"?) "Thank you," he said. "Are you from around here?" What a perfect opening to blow him away with my credentials and expertise in the game of basketball. (He could have said "What time is it?" and I would have worked in my condensed bio sketch somehow.)

I proceeded to give him the Reader's Digest version of all of my basketball achievements. The way I built it up, it sounded like I had just received the Nobel Prize in basketball. Then I gave him a few needed suggestions for the team. I told him if he ever needed any help to let me know.

He didn't need help. He didn't let me know. In fact, he was totally underwhelmed by me. When I came to practice the next week, he hardly acknowledged my pres-

9 1

ence. He didn't implement any of my ideas. Didn't he realize that I had played the game all over the world?

The next day, Bill, who at the same time wanted to get in with the wrestling team, said, "We've got our big opening."

My mind begin to race with all kinds of possibilities. Did they want us to teach classes? Did they want us to lead a Bible study for the wrestling team? Did they need some expert advice on high school students? I looked at Bill and asked, "How do they need our help?" Bill said, "They want us make sure no one brings Cokes in the gym during the state wrestling tournament."

I responded with great agitation, "They want what?" Which translated meant: "You are telling me, a person who knows so much about high school students, basketball, and God, that my big opening on this campus is to make sure no one brings Cokes in the gymnasium?!"

Bill could tell that I had a hard time grasping this. To help me out, he said, "Well, that's not all they want us to do." I responded indignantly, "I should think not." He went on: "They also want us to make sure no one sneaks in without paying."

Later I diagnosed my problem as "The Following Misconception." This is when what you think it means to follow Christ and what Christ thinks it means to follow Him are totally different. I realized that either I needed to rethink some major attitudes in my life, or God needed to change some key passages of Scripture. After several days of attitude adjustment, God gave me three insights from Matthew 20:25-28.

> Jesus called them together and said, "You know that the rulers of the Gentiles lord it over them, and their high officials exercise authority over them. Not so with you. Instead, whoever wants to become great among you must be your servant, and whoever wants to be first must be your slave—just as the Son of Man did not come to be served, but to serve, and to give his life as a ransom for many" (Matthew 20:25-28).

Actually, these are more like obvious-sights rather than insights.

OBVIOUS-SIGHT #1

Serving doesn't come naturally. Naturally I desire for someone to serve me. I want to impress people with my authority. But Jesus said, "You know the rulers of the Gentiles lord it over them and their high officials exercise authority over them. Not so with you" (vv. 25-26). I had forgotten that, unlike the world, Jesus has given me the privilege to serve.

OBVIOUS-SIGHT #2

Serving identifies me with Jesus. I saw serving as demeaning. But Jesus saw it as greatness. He said, "Whoever wants to be great among you must be your servant" (v. 26). In his book *Improving Your Serve*, Charles Swindoll says "We are never more like God than when we serve."[1]

"We are never more like God than when we serve." Charles Swindoll

OBVIOUS-SIGHT #3

Serving gets me inside the school. Why did Jesus say, "Instead, whoever wants to become great among you must be your servant, and whoever wants to be first must be your slave. . ." (vv. 26-27)? He said it because, humanly speaking, everyone wants to be great and to be first. But to become "great" and "first" in other peoples' eyes, we must serve them, not use them.

The old saying holds true in this context: "People don't care how much you know, until they know how much you care." Students and administrators don't care about our expertise, our impressive resumes, or our programs. They will respond to someone who is "great" enough to serve. The coach I tried to impress didn't need another know-it-all on the court. He needed someone to help him do his job better, whether it meant coaching or cleaning up wet spots on the floor. Making sure no one brought Cokes into the gym at the wrestling tournament began to help me see God's way. By manning the ticket table for hours, cleaning trash, washing sweat off the mats, I could serve as the Son of Man served. When I did that, the Lord opened the doors to that school wide and far. The faculty and the administration loved us. The basketball coach asked if I would help with the team. The track coach practically begged us to help him with the track team. When we served, God moved!

Through serving, you build relationships. In the eyes of the faculty and administration, you become a friend, not a local church youth leader who has come to prey on these helpless, unsuspecting kids or make the principal's job harder.

Once you make a conscious choice to serve others on the campus, these general "service tips" will help you in your ministry to the campus.

SERVE HUMBLY

Selfishly, I ask the question: "How can he serve me?" But the unselfish question that I need to write on my heart is, "How can I serve him?" The Apostle Paul describes Jesus as the perfect example, not of arrogant self-service, but of humble self-giving. Paul wrote that Jesus, "being in the very nature God, did not consider equality with God something to be grasped, but made himself nothing, taking the very nature of a servant" (Philippians 2:6-7). After meditating on this verse, I can ask myself a very practical question: "Do I serve people the way I want to serve them or the way Jesus would serve them?"

For example, what does a first-year teacher need? Certainly not another person giving him advice. Instead, the teacher needs someone humbly willing to support and encourage him. Three penetrating questions will help us sort out whether or not we are serving humbly.
- Do I care about this person?
- Am I here for this person or for me?
- Am I willing to serve no matter how great the inconvenience?

SERVE FELT NEEDS

The next question we need to emboss on our brain: "What needs does this person have?" Matthew 4:11 tells us that after Jesus' temptation in the desert, the angels came and attended him. The word attended is used several times in the Bible in the context of meeting someone's felt needs, that is, physical needs. Just as God's heavenly messengers had the privilege of tending to Jesus' physical needs, His earthly messengers have the privilege of tending to the needs of people around them every day. When ministering on the campus, look for opportunities to meet physical needs.

When I first went to the gym, I noticed that the managers had to sweep the floor every day, get the water ready for the team, and tape everyone's ankles. They never seemed to get all of these things done on time. I volunteered to sweep the floor. For two years I came to practice to sweep the floor. Felt needs exist all around us. The observant eye of a servant will reveal them to us quickly.

- Does someone need a ride?
- Do they need someone to sell tickets?
- Does the administration need someone to drive students to events?
- Do students need help with their studies?

And the list of questions and needs goes on. . .

As you observe people at school, ask yourself, *If I were that person, what would I least enjoy doing?* Then volunteer to do it. For the past four years I have helped the managers get everything set up for the football games. During the game, I hand out water to the players. Sometimes when a big, mean tackle knocks a cup out of my hand I ask myself, *Why am I handing out water to these guys who don't even appreciate it? I am too old to take this. Furthermore, I'm probably qualified to coach this team.* When I regain perspective, I answer my own question: Because Jesus would do it.

SERVE IN THE SMALL THINGS

Doing the small things enhances our ministries significantly in several areas. First, it keeps our hearts and motives pure. Anyone can do the glory jobs, but it takes a sincere servant of Christ to do those things that no one else will do.

Second, doing the little things lets people know that we care about them. Attention and recognition come from doing the big things. But a true servant doesn't care whether anybody notices. Doing the small things communicates "I care about you."

Third, doing the small things opens up more opportunities for ministry. Telling the parable of the talents in Matthew 25:14-30, Jesus commends the first two men: "Well done, good and faithful servant! You have been faithful with a few things. I will put you in charge of many things." When we serve faithfully in small ways, God sees that we can be used for His purposes. Then He opens the way for larger opportunities.

When we serve faithfully in small ways,
God sees that we can be used for His purposes.

SERVE SENSITIVELY

Have you ever had someone breathing down your neck, asking what he could do, when you wish he would just leave you alone? We need to serve, but not obnoxiously. The women in Jesus' discipleship band understood that. Matthew describes them as sensitive servers. "Many women were there, watching from a distance. They had followed Jesus from Galilee to care for his needs" (Matthew 27:55). Wait for the right opportunity, a real need the other person has, then "care for his needs."

SERVE "THE LEAST"

One philosophy and attitude of youth ministry has floated around for years: move with the movers. In other words, get with the key leaders, focus your ministry on them, then all the others will follow. To say it another way, if we reach the haves, then the have-nots will follow. Let's face it, all of us like to reach "the sharp, cool, with-it" students. After several years of following that approach, I began to see that nothing could be further from the biblical truth. In Matthew 25:31-46, Jesus tells the parable of the sheep and the goats. Jesus delivers the application of the parable in verse 40: "I tell you the truth, whatever you did for one of the least of these brothers of mine, you did for me."

Chris managed the football team. A manager isn't exactly the type of person that everyone else in the school admires. Usually the manager is the person who wanted to play but wasn't quite good enough. He certainly won't gain much recognition. The Lord showed me that I needed to serve Chris. During football practice and games, I would help him carry equipment or fix water bottles for the team. Two years later, Chris accepted Christ. Now he serves as an athletic trainer at his college. Chris uses his training skills to share the gospel with the players he serves.

When Jesus spoke of "the least of these," He was referring to people, but even more to an attitude. Jesus challenges us to go after the ones whom others have discarded. Since all the ground is level at the foot of the cross, Jesus looks at them not as "the least" but as "the most."

Jesus challenges us to go after the ones whom others have discarded.

SERVE CONSISTENTLY

The best way to destroy the trust you have built with the school and to shut doors that have opened is to make promises and not follow through. You will lose personal respect as well as opportunities for ministry. If people at school cannot count on you to follow through on what you say, how can they trust you with anything else, especially students' lives? In the parable of the two sons in Matthew 21:28-32, the father had asked each of his sons to go work in the vineyard. The first said no, but later went. The second said yes, but never went. The question is asked: Which one did what the father asked?" The answer: The first one.

As you establish a serving ministry on the campus, you will want to keep this parable in mind, as well as two practical applications from it. First, never make promises you cannot keep. You cannot do everything. Say no when you cannot do what you are asked. To say no rather than yes is your best response when you don't know if you can follow through with the request. That way you won't let the person down. Don't feel that a door may close if you do not do everything everyone at the school asks you to do. In reality, you cannot do everything. On the other hand, you guarantee closed doors if you make promises you can't keep. Second, do what you say, no matter what the cost. Many times I have volunteered for a job that got very tiring. Or after I began, it seemed like a waste of time. Or if no one appreciated it, I wanted to quit. If you said you would do it, then by all means do it with all your heart.

SERVE OPENHANDEDLY

Serving costs. One night we had a group at our house. The carpet installers had finished putting new carpet in our house that day. One of the kids got sick. As he was about to throw up, he panicked and began to run for the bathroom. He puked.

And puked. He couldn't find the bathroom. He puked again. He had strewn vomit from one end of our house to the other!

Before that fateful night, we had made a choice that we would not try to protect our earthly possessions. That decision came from an encounter years earlier with a statement by A. W. Tozer. "He who possesses nothing owns everything."[2]

**"He who possesses nothing owns everything."
A. W. Tozer**

Even though our decision got tested that night, it has been a good choice. In working with young people, give all you can. Don't hold back anything: money, house, car, gas, time. Never serve grudgingly. Kids will see Christ in your life by the way you give.

SERVE LOVINGLY

Recently I took thirty sophomores on a weekend retreat. Merely going through a weekend like that is serving! Honestly, I loved it. And do you know how we closed the weekend? I began to wash their feet. Then they washed each other's feet. In that moment of serving, I realized how much I loved those kids. In John 13:1, Jesus "showed. . .the full extent of this love" by washing the disciples' feet. John 13 vividly pictures what it takes to serve: real love. When we love another person, nothing is too difficult, nothing is beneath us. We simply put on a towel and go after it, just like Jesus did.

In the end, where does this leave us? Hebrews 6:10 says, "God is not unjust; he will not forget your work and the love you have shown him as you have helped his people and continue to help them." God blesses people who do His work, His way. He will open doors you can never imagine.

God blesses people who do His work, His way.

I began serving my campus nine years ago. Three principals have come and gone. Teachers and coaches have appeared and disappeared. Numerous youth workers have arrived but then either gave up or were asked to leave. I have never been asked to leave the campus; in fact, just the opposite has happened. Recently I was asked to serve on a committee of teachers who advise troubled students. I have also been asked by the school board to attend a conference that trains people to lead support groups for troubled students. Frequently I speak at the school in a variety of capacities. I have moved from being an outsider who wanted to spend time on the campus to being an insider who is part of the campus.

Robert Greenleaf summarized in a profound way the stance we need to take:

> There is a new problem in our country. We are becoming a nation that is dominated by large institutions—churches, businesses, governments, labor unions, universities—and these big institutions are not serving us well. I hope that all of you will be concerned about this. Now you can do as I do, stand outside and criticize, bring pressure if you can, write and argue about it. All of this may do some good. But nothing of substance will happen unless people inside these institutions who are able to (and want to) lead them into better performance for the public good. Some of you ought to make careers inside these big institutions and become a force for good—from the inside.[3]

You can change the school from the inside, if you will serve.

TAKING ACTION

Campus Serving Strategy

Reflect on Charles Swindoll's statement: "We are never more like God than when we serve," then complete the "Campus Serving Strategy" for your campus.

1. Since so much about serving is an attitude, Lord I offer You this prayer asking You to make me a servant on the campus.

_____

_____

_____

_____

2. The best place for me to serve is:

(Fill this out from the decision you made in the last chapter.)

_____

3. Which faculty member or student is in charge of this activity?

_____

4. Am I willing to serve this person no matter how much it inconveniences me? Why?

_____

5. Make a list of 10 creative ideas for serving this person.

_____   _____

_____   _____

_____   _____

_____   _____

_____   _____

6. Name three students you know in this group. List one felt need beside each name. Write down one way you can observe that person in order to meet his or her felt needs.

Name   Felt Need   Way to Serve

_____

_____

_____

7. Choose one student in the group with the greatest needs. What one action can you take to begin to meet those needs?

_____

_____

8. Write down ideas for one service project you can do for the group as a whole.

_____

_____

_____

9. Based on the answers to the questions above, write out a plan of action you will take each week for the next month to serve this group.

Week 1

_____

_____

_____

Week 2

_____

_____

_____

Week 3

_____

_____

_____

Week 4

_____

_____

_____

NOTES

1. Charles Swindoll, *Improving Your Serve* (Waco, Tex.: Word, 1982), 52.

2. A. W. Tozer, *The Pursuit of God* (Harrisburg. Pa.: Christian Publications, Inc., 1948), 52.

3. Robert K. Greenleaf, *Servant Leadership* (New Yorlc Paulist Press, 1977), 1,2.

PART THREE

LOVE STUDENTS TO CHRIST

SEVEN

BECOME FRIENDS WITH KIDS

"Hey, who is that nerd in the leisure suit?"

The story goes that during an inner city riot, the bombing, looting, and destruction created havoc in the neighborhood. One young girl woke up in the night frightened by all of the noise. Her mother was still at work. She found herself all alone. That made her even more afraid. She cried out for her mother, but no one answered. After what seemed like an eternity, her mother came home. The little girl told her how frightened she was. Her mother comforted her, then said, "I know you were afraid, but remember, God was here with you." The little girl replied, "But mamma, I needed someone with skin on."

By going on the campus, our presence makes us like God "with skin on." We go on campus for the purpose of building relationships with students. We want them to understand that God incarnated Himself in Jesus Christ, died, rose again, and now can change their lives. God desires to express that message through us. Joe Aldrich expressed it this way: "God's communication strategy has always been to wrap an idea in a person."[1] If we have taken all of the necessary steps to get on the campus, but don't know how to build relationships with students, then we won't accomplish our ultimate objective: to lead young people to Jesus Christ.

Not knowing how to build those kinds of relationships can make us feel very insecure. Having been out of high school for a longtime, I walked onto the campus the first time with no idea what I was doing. A fish out of water would be a good description. Everybody knew I was not a student. Wearing jeans and a T-shirt, I was obviously not a teacher. Without a mop or broom, nobody mistook me for the janitor either.

Vividly entrenched in my memory is the moment I walked into the gym. I felt as though every eye was staring at me, and I thought they were asking "Who is that bozo?" To make matters worse, when I walked up to a group of students to introduce myself, they backed away from me like I had mega-bad breath. After an hour of playing human anti-magnets, repelling everyone in sight, I drove home feeling like a total failure. Everywhere I had gone, people took off the other way. *What is wrong with me? Maybe being an accountant wouldn't be so bad after all.* I felt like the Rodney Dangerfield of youth ministry: I didn't get any respect. These students didn't care that I had sacrificed my valuable time so they could have eternal life. In fact, they didn't even care that I existed.

But thankfully for me and the taxpaying public, I didn't go into accounting. In a crash course on building relationships, I learned how to become friends with kids.

In John 4:1-42 Jesus shows us how to build friendships so we can dynamically share His love with students.

GET A GRIP ON WHO YOU ARE AND WHAT YOU ARE DOING

Tucked in the heart of this story of the woman at the well, we find the clue to Jesus' ability to relate to people.

> Meanwhile his disciples urged him, "Rabbi, eat something."
>
> But he said to them, "I have food to eat that you know nothing about."
>
> Then his disciples said to each other, "Could someone have brought him food?"
>
> "My food," said Jesus, "is to do the will of him who sent me and to finish his work." (John 4:31-34).

Jesus' basic motivation for doing the Father's will and finishing His work needs to become our motivation in building relationships on the campus.

KNOW WHO YOU ARE

Jesus had an incredible grasp on His self-image. No identity crisis here! He said, "I have food to eat that you know nothing about" (v. 32). That statement reveals that He knew His roots and His resources. He called Himself "the Son of Man" (John 1:51) and "the Son of God" (see John 3:16-18). He knew where He came from and where He was going.

To have confidence on the campus you must realize who you are. You are not a teacher, an administrator, a student, the maintenance staff, or a security guard. And you are not a person hanging around just because you don't have anything else to do. At times people will look at you as though you are from another planet.

At times people will look at you as though you are from another planet.

From their perspective you don't belong on their campus. When you get this what-planet-are-you-from stare, remember: You represent another Kingdom. You are an ambassador for Jesus Christ (2 Corinthians 5:20). Each time I go on campus, I remember 1 Peter 2:9: "But you are a chosen people, a royal priesthood, a holy nation, a people belonging to God, that you may declare the praises of him who called you out of darkness into his wonderful light." That helps me deal with those who-the-heck-are-you stares.

KNOW THE SIGNIFICANCE OF YOUR MISSION

From Jesus' statement "My food is to do the will of him who sent me and to finish his work," we can tell that Jesus had His purpose eternally inscribed on His heart: to do the will of His Father. This purpose so intensely consumed Him that it even served as His nourishment.

Can you remember the last time you forgot to eat? You may have to tax your brain on this one. What so engrossed you that you didn't even take time to eat? When you immerse yourself in the will of God, everything else becomes secondary. When you possess that kind of intensity and single-mindedness, young people will be attracted to you. They will want to know what makes you tick. And they will realize that your sense of mission makes everything you do important, whether they understand it or not.

KNOW WHO IS IN CONTROL

Imagine Jesus saying: "Well, I don't know, Peter, that last town was pretty tough. What if these folks don't accept me as being the Messiah either? I mean, the next thing you know, no one will believe I am the Messiah. Then I'm really in trouble. Everyone will think I made all this up. My name could be mud." No, not Jesus. His Father started the work and had willed that Jesus would complete it. Nothing could derail that plan. Jesus had confidence because He knew that God had everything under control.

You will save yourself great amounts of emotional energy if you realize that God started the work on your campus and that He will complete it. In the process He will use you. Nothing a principal, teacher, or student says or does can derail God's plan for that campus. God has everything under control.

Nothing a principal, teacher, or student says or does can derail God's plan for that campus.

GO WHERE OTHERS REFUSE TO GO

Going back to the beginning of John 4, we see Jesus' ingenious ability to build a positive relationship with the woman at the well. John writes that Jesus "had to go through Samaria" (v. 4). The Jews and the Samaritans detested each other, carrying on a continual feud of anger, resentment, and hatred. The Jews considered the Samaritans half-breeds, because, as Jews, they had married pagans and mixed other religious practices with the worship of Jehovah. Therefore, the Jews had virtually no dealings with the Samaritans and even avoided going through Samaria. But not Jesus. He headed directly into the place where everyone else refused to go.

Think about what Jesus was walking into there. He was not welcome. He did not fit in. He had no relationships with anyone there. He stuck out like a sore thumb. Jesus' experience in Samaria is similar to what it is like to go on campus the first time. It is not for the fainthearted.

To go where others refuse to go, we need to discover where kids hang out. Then, like Jesus, instead of walking around those places, we go right through them. Try this out in one of these two situations.

Athletic Events. Resist the temptation to sit with the parents. Look for a seat right in the middle of the student section. Often, students don't come to watch the game, but to socialize. This provides you with a great forum to talk. At halftime, students will leave the stands and congregate near the concession stand. It's called the I-want-to-make-sure-I'm-not-missing-anything exodus. If you hang around there, you won't miss anything either.

After-school Hangouts. The best time to meet new students is immediately after school, as soon as the last bell rings. For all of the complaining they do about school, kids certainly like to hang around after the bell. And usually they hang around the same general area every day. They gravitate to their comfort zone, where their friends hang out; namely:

- the bus stop
- the locker rooms
- the athletic practice field and gym
- the smoking area
- the student parking lot
- in front of the school.

Find out where students you know go and show up there. For example, some of the guys I am trying to reach play slam dunk basketball with an eight-foot goal at a friend's house every day. I go there. Check out the arcades, the malls, and the fast-food restaurants. Listen when they talk to find out what the students you know do after school.

At first this will seem awkward and unnatural. But like learning to do anything else, if you persist, you will become very comfortable and natural in penetrating student hangouts.

PERSEVERE WITH A PURPOSE

As Jesus moved through Samaria in the heat of the day, He realized how weary He was. John writes, "Jesus, tired as he was from the journey, sat down by the well" (John 4:6). Out of His own need, Jesus met the Samaritan woman. He could have drawn His own water or taken her water and left. Instead, even in His weariness and thirst, he met her.

Many days you will have distractions and interruptions that will keep you from going to the campus. Some days you will want to say, "Forget it, I'm not going to that school today." Other days you will leave from the school and say, "I'm never going back there again." Like Jesus, we get tired in ministry. Sometimes we will want to quit. Let's be honest: It takes incredible amounts of spiritual, mental, and emotional energy for ministry, especially to kids. At times you will need a break from continually meeting new people and spending time relating to them. Once you get a needed break, I challenge you: persevere.

PLAY NO FAVORITES

Even though Jesus knew that Jews and Samaritans despised each other, still He entered into a triple-whammy social no-no. He struck up a conversation with a Samaritan (Whammy #1). Not only was she a Samaritan, but she was a woman as well. It was a strict social custom that a man should never speak to a woman (Whammy #2). Then he asked to drink from her cup. By drinking after a Samaritan, who also was a woman, Jesus not only risked His health (as social custom believed) but also destroyed His social standing (Whammy #3).

Just as Jesus faced these social barriers, we will face social barriers on the school campus. Often unspoken, these stubbornly defined lines are not to be crossed. Preppies don't associate with metal heads; yuppies with blue collars; "brains" with "airheads"; athletes with drama types; blacks with whites or whites with Hispanics, punkers with anyone. In the midst of social barriers and social pressure, we must remember that Jesus plays no favorites.

We must remember that Jesus plays no favorites.

The constant challenge on the campus is to break through these barriers to build relationships with all types of students, not based on common interests, but on the love God has for them. To do this...

* Understand that all students search desperately for someone who cares enough

1 1

to break through these walls to touch their lives.

- Realize that these exterior social walls protect tender hearts that are trying desperately to find their places in life and not get hurt in the process.

- Grasp that God wants you to love all students regardless of their social status.

INITIATE RELATIONSHIPS

When the Samaritan woman came to the well "Jesus said to her... ." (John 4:7). Jesus could have let the opportunity pass. After all, He was tired. No one would have noticed or cared. Because of the social situation, no one would have said, "What a rude Jew not to talk to that woman." However, Jesus didn't take the easy way out. He initiated a relationship.

Today, in our non-interactive society, we don't have to speak to the people around us. We consider not speaking to be normal. However, like Jesus, we have the privilege of initiating caring conversations, knowing that each person we talk to is a divine appointment. Use the following tips to sharpen your conversational kills.

1. *Take a partner along with you.* This will help you not to feel awkward and alone.

2. *Never stand around by yourself.* Even if you don't know kids, walk up to them and ask questions - even if the only question you can think of is "Where's the bathroom?" Memorize questions to open a conversation. Some people converse naturally, but for those of us who struggle with it, you can use these questions:
- What time is it?
- What is your name? ("Hi, my name is Tim. What's yours?")
- When is the next ball game?
- What activities at school do you like?
- Who leads the choir, drama, etc.?
- Where did you get that T-shirt?

Remember, students enjoy talking about their interests, not yours.

3. *Never call a person by a generic nickname.* Names like Bud, Pal, Sport, Bubba or their equivalents should be avoided when initiating a relationship. Walking into

a meeting once, I saw a person whom I had seen before coming toward me, so I said, "Hey, bud, how are you doing?" A friend who was with me started laughing. "Bud" wasn't a "bud" after all, but a girl who gave me the nastiest stare. That was not a good move for relationship building.

4. *Remember names.* Since remembering names provides such a positive key to building relationships, you can use these clues to help you do that more effectively.

- Repeat the name. As soon as a person tells you his name, repeat that name in your mind three times, then use it in the conversation three times.

- Commit the name to memory. To do this, imagine the person you have just met is a friend of yours by the same name. For example, if I meet John, I imagine him walking together with my other friend named John. Then the next time I see my new friend John at school, I will think of him with my old friend John, and I will remember that his name is John. This little plan works great until you meet somebody named Melchizedek!

- Write the name down. As soon as you leave that person, write his name down. Jot it in your journal. Which journal? The one you will start keeping now that was mentioned earlier in the book!

- Keep a journal. Buy a journal that you keep handy. When you get in your car to leave the campus, pull out your journal. Write down all of the information you can remember about each student you met. Note a brief description of looks and any particular needs you could detect. Update this page as you find out more about that person. Photocopy his or her picture from of the yearbook, newspaper, or school program and tape it on that page in your journal.

- Pray for each one. Using your journal as a prayer reminder, pray for the students with whom you want to build relationships.

BE YOURSELF

The rule of thumb in the *How to Avoid Samaritans at All Costs* handbook: "Never admit a need." Obviously, Jesus never read that handbook because He asked the Samaritan woman, "Will you give me a drink?" (v. 7). Jesus not only admitted He had a need, He asked this woman to meet it. His vulnerability and transparency caused people to open up to Him. He never tried to impress people or to get them to like Him. Very simply, He acted as we would expect Jesus to act. He acted like Himself.

Just as Jesus expressed His needs and allowed others to meet them, we need to respond to kids with the same kind of transparency and vulnerability. Someone who tries to impress kids with how "together" his life is or how "spiritual" he is, doesn't get very far with students because, even better than adults, they can see through all of that. When we let them in on our needs they will be attracted rather than repelled. Students will want to be around us because we are real.

In building relationships with young people, God intends for you to be yourself. The last thing kids need is for you to act like a student. You can relax in God's Spirit and be yourself. When you do that; the life and love of Jesus will flow through you because God enjoys using a real, transparent person to reveal Himself.

PENETRATE DEFENSE MECHANISMS

The Samaritan woman had her defenses up, and she said to Jesus, "You are a Jew and I am a Samaritan woman. How can you ask me for a drink?" (v. 9). With an uncanny ability to discern defensiveness, Jesus went to the heart of the matter. "If you knew the gift of God and who it is that asks for a drink, you would have asked him and he would have given you living water" (v. 10).

Much like the Samaritan woman, many students come across as tough and defensive. Yet behind the toughness we discover tender, hurting hearts that desperately want love and compassion. Often those young hearts have experienced abuse. They cry out: "Don't hurt me anymore!" They protect themselves by building defensive walls so no one can hurt them again.

For that reason, they test you to see if you care. They want to know your angle. Often the people in their lives don't care about them, but do want something from them. Therefore, their first instinct is to find out what you want. They do this by rejecting you. Is that weird? Yes, but they reason that if you really care about them, you will not leave when they reject you. If you are real, you will continue to come back. If you are not real, you will give up after a few cold shoulders. Don't let this test throw you off! Follow these "rejection resistors" and you will not get hurt when you run into their walls of defensiveness.

If you are real, you will continue to go back.

- Never take rejection personally.
- Expect apathy. Apathy is "in."
- Realize that their reactions attempt to hide their hurt.
- Keep coming back until they know that you care.

Now that you have built up some "rejection resistance," let's find some ways to tear down the walls in these kids' lives.

- Speak to them every time you see them. Stop. Look them in the eye. Listen to what they say. Even if you communicate for only 15 to 20 seconds, you will express how much you care.

- Support them in their activities. Show up at a ball game or other events that involve them.

- Notice their achievements, and let them know you've noticed.

- Never promise something you cannot do. If they invite you to attend an event, and you say you will come, then do it. If you can't attend, don't be afraid to say that. If something comes up that causes you to have to cancel, call and let them know ahead of time. That way they will know that you cared enough to call.

- Ask the Holy Spirit to shine through you. As your light shines, students will be drawn to that light, and they will want to hear the gospel.

USE CONVERSATIONS TO BUILD CLOSE RELATIONSHIPS

Jesus knew how to develop a conversation and then take it deeper. In John 4:9-14, Jesus took the conversation from the superficial level of asking for a drink to telling the Samaritan woman about Living Water that would give her eternal life. Jesus built conversation bridges with her. We can build these same kind of conversation bridges with students. The bridges focus on their interests. Students love to talk about themselves.

Students love to talk about themselves.

When you meet with students, listen carefully. Then take the topic that seems most important to them at the time and discuss it on increasingly deeper levels than the time before. You can keep tabs on this information in your journal. Let's walk through an example.

CONVERSATION #1

I met Bob at school. In the conversation I asked him, "How long have you lived in Atlanta?" Bob mentioned that he moved to Atlanta recently because his parents got a divorce. He lives with his mom. His dad lives in Florida. (This is Level #1: Ask information questions.)

CONVERSATION #2

When I saw Bob again I asked: "Bob, how's your Mom doing living on her own?" From this question I found out more about Bob and his family. He said, "We do OK. Dad's pretty good about sending money, but it's still hard on Mom having to raise the four of us." (This is Level #2: Ask probing questions.)

CONVERSATION #3

The next day I saw Bob again, and we talked some more. I said "Bob, I know that not seeing your dad must be tough. How do you feel about your relationship with your dad?" Bob said, "I've just kind of given up on him being around. He has a family of his own now, so I don't see him much."

At this point I have discerned not only what his family life is like, but also what feelings he has about his family. I got a glimpse of his relationship with his dad and mom; where he hurts in regard to his family; and his view of God, even though he didn't mentioned God's name. (This is Level #3: Ask feeling questions.)

CONVERSATION #4

In my next encounter with Bob, I said, "Bob, I have never experienced my mom and dad breaking up, but I imagine it's pretty painful. How are you dealing with all you have gone through?" Bob told me, "I just do the best I can. I've made it through all the tough times so far, so I guess I'll make it through the rest." Through these conversations the relationship has developed to the point that Bob will probably be open to hearing the gospel. (This is Level #4: Ask gospel introduction questions. In the next chapter we will discuss how to do that.)

You get the idea. The conversations should get deeper each time until the student is thirsty for Living Water.

BUILD A NETWORK OF NEW RELATIONSHIPS

From a simple stop to get a drink of water to a whole town wanting Living Water. That's amazing progress! John writes:

> Then, leaving her water jar, the woman went back to the town and said to the people, "Come, see a man who told me everything I ever did. Could this be the Christ?" They came out of the town and made their way toward him (John 4:28.30).

When people encounter Jesus, word tends to get out! Like the Samaritan woman and all of her needy friends, students thirst for Jesus Christ. The God-shaped vacuum longs to be filled in each one. When someone cares for them and genuinely gives them the Living Water, you can count on it: THEY WILL BRING THEIR FRIENDS.

That gives you multiplied opportunities to build relationships. In fact, a network of relationships will develop. It will take all the time you can give to keep up with the opportunities you will have. As this develops, I recommend three steps of action:

1. Set a goal of having a meaningful, "moving-toward-the-gospel" conversation every time you met.

2. Train students who began a relationship with Christ to share their faith with their friends. (See chapter 11.)

3. Call on your Leadership Team and your maturing Christian students in disci-

116

pleship groups to help you meet the relationship needs. Unless you follow through on this one, you will get overwhelmed with relationships quickly.

GIVE FREELY OF YOUR TIME

Nothing communicates love more than time.

Jesus understood the value of giving time in building relationships. He took time to show people like the Samaritan woman and her friends that He cared. "So when the Samaritans came to him, they urged him to stay with them, and he stayed two days. And because of his words many more became believers" (John 4:40).

Unhurried, uninterrupted, un-I-have-more-important-things-to-do time expresses love. In the art of building relationships, nothing substitutes for time.

Scott and I spent three months talking about very little other than whether or not a particular girl liked him. It seemed like a waste of time to me. I thought this guy had girls on the brain 24/7. However, out of that time investment, Scott came to Christ. Later he became an intern in our youth ministry. Now that he has graduated from college, he is investing his life in reaching young people and training youth leaders in Eastern Europe. Every second spent with Scott was worth it. Scott's story challenges us not to give up in building relationships.

By daily giving of ourselves, going where we don't seem to fit, engaging in awkward conversations, breaking through walls of hurt and resentment, spending time with kids, and showing that we care, we will bring many to drink fully of the Living Water.

TAKING ACTION

A Strategy for Building Relationships on Campus

Applying the principles we discovered in John 4, design a step-by-step approach for reaching non-Christian students.

GET A GRIP ON WHO YOU ARE AND WHAT YOU ARE DOING

KNOW WHO YOU ARE

Imagine walking on the campus for the first time with kids staring at you. Write one sentence that you want to carry with you to remind you of who you are.

_____

_____

_____

KNOW THE SIGNIFICANCE OF YOUR MISSION

Again, you are walking on the campus for the first time. State clearly your mission.

_____

_____

_____

KNOW WHO IS IN CONTROL

As you envision yourself walking on the campus, write one sentence that will remind you Who is in control.

_____

_____

_____

Now take these three sentences and write them in one easy-to-remember sentence. Repeat it until you have memorized it, then carry it on campus with you. It's your campus mission statement.

_____

_____

_____

GO WHERE OTHERS REFUSE TO GO

Identify one group of students that you want to get to know.

_____

Where do they hang out?

_____

_____

What approach will you use to get to know them?

_____

_____

_____

PERSEVERE WITH A PURPOSE

In order to persevere, determine when you will go to the campus consistently.

The days of the week:

_____

The hours of those days:

_____

PLAY NO FAVORITES

To what kind of kids do you have the most difficult time relating? Write out a plan to get to know one of those kids.

_____

_____

_____

INITIATE RELATIONSHIPS

Who will you partner with to go on campus?

_____

Formulate the series of questions that you will ask when you go on campus the first time. Have these clearly in mind.

_____

_____

_____

_____

___Check here when you have set up your journal.

What key idea do you want to use to remember names?

_____

_____

Write the names of three young people you would like to get to know.

1.

2.

3.

BE YOURSELF

What personal needs do you have that you can share with kids?

_____

_____

_____

PENETRATE DEFENSE MECHANISMS

What specific actions will you take to break through defense mechanisms?

1.

2.

3.

USE CONVERSATIONS TO BUILD CLOSE RELATIONSHIPS

Keeping in mind one student with whom you want to build a relationship, write four questions you will use to move a series of conversations toward the gospel.

1.

2.

3.

4.

BUILD A NETWORK OF NEW RELATIONSHIPS

Write down the name of one student who is not a Christian. Then write down the names of as many of his friends as you know. Let the list grow.

_____

_____

_____

_____

_____

KEEP ON GIVING YOUR TIME! IT WILL PAY OFF!

NOTES

1. Joseph C. Aldrich, *Gentle Persuasion: Creative Ways to Introduce Your Friends to Christ* (Portland, Ore.: Barna Multnomah Press, 1988), 49.

EIGHT

COMMUNICATE THE MESSAGE OF CHRIST

"You mean you really would like to know Jesus?"

I looked Billy in the eyes and said, "Billy, does this make sense to you?" He nodded yes. I then asked him, "Has anyone ever shared this with you before?" He replied, "Never." The previous half hour of conversation over a Coke and curly fries had led to this point. He had expressed amazement that God actually wanted a personal relationship with Him. "With so many people in the world, why would God want to know me?" At one point in the conversation I asked him if he was ready to accept Christ. As we talked I could tell he was not ready. He wasn't sure if he could give God certain areas of his life. I asked Billy to read the Gospel of John and to write down his questions. As I drove him home I prayed that God would open the door of Billy's heart so he would understand the love of Jesus for him. Billy and I talked often, but I never pressed him about his relationship to Christ.

Four months passed. One Sunday night Billy showed up at a discussion session. After listening to these students talk for over an hour, I explained what it would mean to ask Christ into their lives. I encouraged those who were ready to talk to me afterwards. As I walked outside, Billy came up behind me and said, "I'm ready now." With tears in his eyes he opened his heart to Jesus. As I drove home I kept thinking, "It doesn't get any better than this."

We discovered the dynamics of cultivating a relationship in the last chapter. In this chapter we want to focus on how to sow the seed of the gospel in cultivated soil. How can we communicate the message of Christ in the context of a relationship?

If we cultivate the soil but never sow the seed in students' lives, we not only miss the point, but the opportunity as well.

To discover how to sow the seed more effectively, let's continue observing Jesus as He sowed the seed from five "seed bags" with the Samaritan woman.

SEED BAG #1
BUILD A PLATFORM FOR POSITIVE COMMUNICATION

In the encounter with the Samaritan woman, we see how Jesus created an atmosphere for good communication. John 4:6-7 tells us,

> Jesus, tired as he was from the journey, sat down by the well. It was about the sixth hour. When a Samaritan woman came to draw water, Jesus said to her, "Will you give me a drink?"

In a relaxed manner, Jesus asked for a drink. Then privately He encouraged the Samaritan woman to talk openly about her life. Jesus built a platform for good conversation.

To create this same kind of environment with students we need to set up appointments properly. Setting up an appointment may seem easy enough, yet one of the questions youth leaders ask the most is, "How do I set up an appointment with a student without him thinking I'm some kind of weirdo?" It can be awkward or comfortable, depending on how you handle it. These steps will help make it easier.

"How do I set up an appointment with a student without him thinking I'm some kind of weirdo?"

1. *Block out times in your schedule to meet students.* Students have busy schedules, and so do you. Block out times for appointments. I have three blocks of time a week for appointments: two afternoons after school and all day Saturday. Bend your schedule as much as you can to meet the student's situation.

2. *Decide on a private location, but not a secluded one.* Find a place where the

student will feel comfortable to talk freely. Stay away from formal places, like your office. On the other hand, stay away from places that are too informal, like the school hangout. Find a place that he considers special, a nice restaurant where kids would like to go. At a place like this students feel comfortable and special, and you have fewer distractions.

3. *Never meet with the opposite sex alone.* Youth ministry has lost some great leaders because they put themselves in compromising situations. Remember: Avoid even the appearance of evil. If you have to meet with the opposite sex, take a leader of the opposite sex with you.

4. *Extend the invitation.* Once you have cultivated a relationship, students will want to spend time with you. All you have to do is ask: "How about a Coke after school?"

5. *Give the reason.* If a student asks "What's up?" have a reason. Say "I want to get to know you better." Once in a while I get a no. That let's me know that I need to spend more time building the relationship.

6. *Confirm the appointment.* When you set the appointment, get a phone number—preferably a cell phone number—in case a problem arises. Call the night before to confirm the appointment. Without a call you have about a 25 percent chance that the student will remember your meeting and show up. But with the call you increase your percentage to 75 percent—yes, only 75 percent. Chances are the student will forget or schedule something else of utmost importance, like going to the mall. Most young people just don't have the hang of those hand held computers yet.

7. *Arrive 15 minutes early.* If you usually arrive late, remember that students will not wait for an adult longer than five minutes, if that much. If you don't arrive early and wait for the student, he will find something else to do pretty quickly. The last thing you want to communicate is that another adult has forgotten him.

8. *NEVER miss an appointment.* If you want to wipe out all your hard work in relationship-building, forget an appointment. The student may say outwardly that it's OK, but inwardly he will feel like you didn't care. It will take extra effort to regain the lost trust.

9. *Pay for the food.* Have you ever met a student who doesn't love a free meal?

Following these simple, practical steps will create the platform for students to open up.

SEED BAG # 2
CREATE AN ATMOSPHERE
OF LOVE AND ACCEPTANCE

Jesus asked the Samaritan woman for a drink, disarming her, causing her to relax (John 4:7). And as the conversation proceeded, He communicated love and acceptance until she felt so comfortable that she said, "Give me this water so I won't get thirsty. . ."(v. 15).

When a student senses that you have more concern for getting his life straightened out than for loving him, he will become defensive instead of hearing what you say. Attempt to build an atmosphere of love and acceptance. Here's how.

1. *Listen intently.* Spend the first 15 or 20 minutes asking the student questions about himself. Instead of talking about your interests, let him know of your interest in him. Instead of thinking about a comment you want to make, focus on what he says, then ask more questions. Make mental notes of what he says.

2. *Ask open-ended questions.* Closed questions begin with *are, is, will, do, has,* and *can.* Such questions are answered with a yes or a no. Try to avoid them. Ask questions that begin with *who, what, where, when, why,* and *how.* For example, if spring break is not far away, you could ask these questions:
  • "Where are you going for spring break?"
  • "What will you do?"
  • "Who will you stay with?"
  • "What is it like there?"

3. *Encourage the expression of feelings.* When a student opens up and tells you something like, "My mom and dad are separated," then encourage him to express his feelings. "What did you feel like when that happened?" "What did you say to your parents?" "How did you find the strength to deal with it?"

Students yearn for someone to love and accept them. If they sense you do, they will allow you to share the message of Christ. You will have created an atmosphere of openness.

Students yearn for someone to love and accept them.

SEED BAG #3
TURN THE CONVERSATION
TO CHRIST

When Jesus talked with the Samaritan woman, He didn't jump right in with, "Give me three good reasons why you shouldn't go to hell." Rather, he had a concern for her needs. He let those needs lead her to the well of Living Water.

> Jesus answered, "Everyone who drinks this water will be thirsty again, but whoever drinks the water I give him will never thirst. Indeed, the water I give him will become in him a spring of water welling up to eternal life" (John 4: 13-14).

Although we know that Jesus meets every need, we also know the difficulty we have in trusting Him with our needs. Multiply that ten times over for a non-Christian, and it's not hard to understand why people find it difficult to "take their first drink." Only when they know that you care about their needs will they listen to your solutions. You can turn the conversation to Christ as you surface their needs.

1. Find a felt need. Our needs usually appear in what we talk about the most. Listen for the topic of conversation that comes up again and again. As you listen and probe, look for negative comments that the student makes about himself. Listen, too, for what he does not say. Often you will discover felt needs in those painful subjects that the person struggles to talk about.

My friend John lived in a foster home. Several times in our conversations he said in various ways that he couldn't wait to get a job so he could get out on his own. That told me he wanted out of his home because things weren't going well with his foster parents.

Discern the felt need, then focus your conversation around that need.

2. Whet the student's appetite. Notice how Jesus' conversation with the Samaritan woman was so enticing that she practically begged him to give her "this water" (v.

15). What Jesus said revived her hope for a solution in her life. He stirred in her an innate desire to quench her thirst with something more, something deeper.

Try to create that kind of thirst in your conversations. Students, like the Samaritan woman, fatalistically accept things as they are, often losing sight of any solutions. Consider my friend John, who lived in the foster home. When I discovered that his father had deserted him, I said, "It must be tough living without your dad, always wondering where he is. You know, John, I think I can help you with this situation." With this statement I created hope. He wanted to know more and he began to have a thirst to find answers. Students will tune in when we hone in on their needs. From those needs we can whet their appetite with the promise of a solution.

3. Move to his real need. After the Samaritan woman asked Jesus for the living water, He did something very interesting. Instead of telling her "I'm it! It's me! Don't you see? I'm the Water of Life! Open your eyes!" He said, "Go call your husband." Go call your husband? Are you kidding me? Wake up, Jesus, before she gets away. You had her in the palm of your hand! She was right there—ready to say the big prayer. And you say, "Go call your husband"!

I don't know about you, but when someone shows interest like the Samaritan woman did, I start drooling. Let's get her into the Kingdom—quick! But Jesus wasn't concerned with notches on his Bible belt or the number of souls saved. He was concerned about her life. She had lived with five men. Her problem wasn't getting a drink of water; she had a relationship void. She desperately wanted a deep relationship but obviously didn't know how to have one. Jesus brought up the subject of the five husbands to help her feel in an even more poignant way her deeper need for a love relationship with the Living God. She knew then that Jesus was the Living Water. Only He could fill that relationship void in her life.

Let's go back to my friend John. I said to him, "John, tell me about your life when your dad was home. Was it ever happy?" John told me that although he loved his dad, his home wasn't all that great. His father had abused his sister. Things had always been tough. In fact, it couldn't have gotten much worse. That's why John hoped that things would be different when he got out on his own.

As we continued to talk, I kept asking questions that helped him see that everything he had counted on wasn't giving him meaning in his life. By the time we finished this conversation, John knew something was missing and that he wasn't going to find it with his present resources.

Only when this happens can we share the gospel effectively.

Even if it takes numerous conversations, we must take students to a point where they see their needs and the inadequacy of their own resources to meet those needs.

Even if it takes numerous conversations, we must take students to a point where they see their needs and their own inadequacy to meet those needs.

SEED BAG #4: RELATE YOUR EXPERIENCE

After Jesus had helped the Samaritan woman see her real need, she realized her plight. And like most people, she thought she had to meet that need through religion. She said, "I can see you are a prophet. Our fathers worshipped on this mountain, but you Jews claim that the place where we must worship is in Jerusalem" (John 4:19).

All the Samaritan woman knew of religion was the external do's and don'ts. That God gives Himself without any conditions to anyone who will receive Him startles people who have been brought up to believe that they have to earn everything they get. Religion is the way they think they can earn favor with God. They focus on rules and behavior rather than on a loving, intimate relationship with Jesus Christ.

The real answer to the woman's spiritual need had nothing to do with religion but everything to do with a fresh, new relationship with the living God. Jesus addressed this clearly (v. 24): "God is Spirit, and his worshippers must worship him in spirit and in truth." What matters is that the Spirit of God can live in us. He is not external, but internal. He can get inside of you where you hurt the most and fill your deepest need.

This concept came to the Samaritan woman with freshness. And it comes that same way to people today. We want to help students avoid religion and discover a fresh, vital, life-changing relationship with Jesus.

We want to help students discover a fresh, vital, life-changing relationship with Jesus.

HELPFUL HINTS

At this point we want to communicate to students with intensity that God Almighty wants to take up residence in their lives. Your story, telling what God has done in your life, provides the most powerful tool to do this. As you prepare to tell your personal story, keep in mind the following hints. They will help you identify with non-Christians and relate your experience in the most effective way.

1. *Begin with an interesting, attention-grabbing sentence.*

2. *Make one Scripture reference the centerpiece of your presentation.* Don't use more than two or three when telling your story.

3. *Build your story around a theme.* Focus on a theme such as self-image, broken family, dashed dreams, life's disappointments, the need for love, or a similar issue that led you to the point of conversion.

4. *Don't worry that you have not taken drugs or committed a crime.* Your experience with the love of God communicated in the power of the Holy Spirit will make your testimony very powerful. Tell *YOUR* story.

5. *Express with honesty your problems and difficulties.* Tell about real life experiences that help non-Christian students identify with you.

6. *Be positive.* Avoid negative communication by not . . .
   - making negative statements about the church, organizations, or people.
   - mentioning denominations.
   - preaching to people.
   - speaking in generalities. Instead specific experiences and events from your life.
   - using words that may not be understood by non-Christians (salvation, saved, conversion, filled with the Spirit).
   - talking too long.

7. *Memorize your story.* Study it until you know it so well that you express it nat-

urally. Time it to make certain it falls in the three-minute range.

8. *Share your story in the power of the Holy Spirit.* Ask God to give you enthusiasm as you tell what He has done in your life. *HE WILL USE IT TO IMPACT STUDENTS' LIVES.*

9. *End with a conclusion that makes students want to know more.*

VITAL INGREDIENTS

Following this outline will insure that you include the vital ingredients in your story.

1. YOUR LIFE BEFORE CHRIST

- Focus on one or two problems in your life which show your sinfulness, such as anxiety, feelings of incompleteness or emptiness, or experiences of hopelessness.
- Relate one personal experience that communicates how you felt during that period of time.
- Tell the sequence of events that brought you to a point where you knew you needed God.

2. HOW YOU CAME TO KNOW CHRIST

- Give the specific circumstances surrounding your experience of receiving Christ.
- Tell specifically what you did when you received Christ.

3. HOW JESUS CHANGED YOUR LIFE

- Focus on one specific way your life has changed. Relate that back to the problem you communicated in #1 above. You can add others as appropriate and as time allows.
- Include specific illustrations about the ways your life has changed.

Preparing "my story" will take the hard work and a significant amount of time, but it will give you a basic tool that you can use over and over again with students to lead them to Christ.

SEED BAG #5
SHARE THE GOSPEL

After Jesus told the Samaritan woman that life with God involves a relationship, He told her how He fit into the picture. This drama reached the climax when Jesus revealed his identity.

> The woman said, "I know that Messiah (called Christ) is coming. When he comes, he will explain everything to us." Then Jesus declared, "I who speak to you am he" (John 4:25-26).

How can we communicate the Good News of who Jesus is when we reach this point with young people?

Reach Out Youth Solutions has developed the *Jesus: No Equal* booklet, designed specifically for students. *Jesus: No Equal*, the book, offers students the opportunity to know Jesus better. I designed it for them to have a passionate encounter with the Son of God. For information on ordering (go to www.reach-out.org or call 1-800-473-9456.)

To communicate the gospel powerfully, memorize the booklet, *Jesus: No Equal* and then draw it on a napkin or piece of paper when you present it to a student. But if you take a Christian student with you, use the *Jesus: No Equal* booklet itself so he can see how he can use this tool with his friends when you are not present by simply reading it to another student.

To make the transition from your story to the gospel, ask

- Have you ever experienced a personal, intimate relationship with Jesus Christ like the one I've described?

Then say:

- The Bible tells how a person can experience that kind of personal relationship with God. Would you be interested in knowing how to do that?

I haven't had anyone with whom I have developed a relationship ever say no to this question.

Explain or read the booklet to the student. When you get to the point of praying to receive Christ, ask him, "Can you say this to God and mean it?" If the person can say that, and you discern deep conviction, then lead him in the prayer to accept Christ.

The Apostle Paul speaks about "deep conviction" in 1 Thessalonians 1:4. The evidence of such conviction is a sincere sense of one's own sinfulness and an overwhelming appreciation for what Jesus Christ did on the cross. If these signs are not apparent, then probably that person is not ready to give his life to Christ completely. To determine where that person is, ask two probing questions.

(1) "Do you understand what I just told you?"

(2) "What does this mean to you?"

Listen to the student's response. If he says something like "I try to be good," or "I go to church every Sunday," you can be sure he hasn't grasped the point yet. If the student does understand, he will ask searching questions and not try to prove to you that he is OK. An urgency to find out how he can know God will override the conversation. The student may express a variety of feelings, but when he first comes to grips with the unconditional love of God, he will feel something.

You can get students to say (or pray) just about anything. But it means nothing if the Holy Spirit has not drawn them to the Father. Be patient. Let the Holy Spirit, not you, bring deep conviction. If the student isn't ready, don't push it. Say, "Why don't you think about this for a few days? Then we'll get back together and talk again." That takes the pressure off both of you. If the student seriously wants to follow Christ, then whatever conviction he has will only become more intense in the following days. Before you leave, set up an appointment to talk with him again.

**You can get students to say (or pray) just about anything.
But it means nothing if the Holy Spirit has not drawn them to the Father.**

In the next chapter, we will discover how to keep this person who accepts Christ growing in Christ and plugged into a family of believers.

TAKING ACTION

A Strategy to Communicate the Message of Christ

BUILD A PLATFORM FOR POSITIVE COMMUNICATION

In rethinking the account of the Samaritan woman, jot down some practical points that will help you communicate the message of Christ positively to high school students.

1.

2.

3.

4.

After reviewing the practical points for setting up appointments with a non-Christian student, set up one appointment.

Name:

Time:

Place:

____Check here when the appointment is confirmed.

CREATE AN ATMOSPHERE OF LOVE AND ACCEPTANCE

Before you meet, write down two or three questions you will use to get the student to talk.

1.

2.

3.

TURN THE CONVERSATION TO CHRIST

Jot down two or three questions that will help you find out one of the student's felt needs.

1.

2.

3.

Write down two or three questions to whet the student's appetite.

1.

2.

3.

Now write down two or three questions you will ask to discover the student's real needs.

1.

2.

3.

Pick out the key question in each category, write it on a 3 x 5 card, then use it during one appointment to keep the conversation flowing.

RELATE YOUR EXPERIENCE

Write out your story following the guidelines in this chapter. Prepare it so that you can present it in three minutes. If you have done this before, do it again. Re-doing it will both refresh what you want to communicate and refine your presentation. Use the outline on the next few pages.

1. My life before I met Christ:

_____

_____

_____

_____

_____

_____

_____

_____

2. How I came to know Christ:

_____

_____

_____

_____

_____

_____

_____

_____

3. How Jesus has changed my life:

_____

_____

_____

_____

_____

_____

_____

_____

SHARE THE GOSPEL

Read through the *Jesus: No Equal* booklet several times to prepare yourself to communicate it during your appointment.

____Check here when you have read the *Jesus: No Equal* booklet three times.

Carry out your appointment; then comment on each aspect of the conversation.

BUILDING A PLATFORM FOR POSITIVE COMMUNICATION

Setting up the appointment:

_____

_____

_____

CREATING THE ATMOSPHERE OF LOVE AND ACCEPTANCE

Key question:

_____

_____

_____

_____

TURNING THE CONVERSATION TO CHRIST

This student's felt need:

_____

_____

_____

Whetting this student's appetite:

_____

_____

_____

This student's real need:

_____

_____

_____

_____

RELATING YOUR EXPERIENCE

My story:

_____

_____

_____

_____

_____

_____

_____

_____

_____

_____

_____

_____

_____

_____

_____

_____

_____

_____

_____

_____

_____

_____

SHARING THE GOSPEL

Gospel presentation:

_____

_____

_____

Response:

_____

_____

_____

Changes you will make for the next appointment:

_____

_____

_____

NINE

GET NEW BELIEVERS STARTED

"Why won't this kid grow faster?"

After spending several months building a relationship with Daniel, I seized the opportunity to share the gospel with him over a Coke one day after lifting weights. He took the bait hook, line, and sinker. Or at least it seemed that way. He looked convicted. He acted convicted. He even said the prayer to accept Christ. I believe he was sincere. Yet somehow it didn't seem to click with him. Daniel's "relationship to Christ" never went further than that salvation prayer and The Lord's Prayer before football games.

On the other hand, Stuart came from a nominally Christian background. His parents had no particular interest in spiritual matters. However, when I told him about Jesus, he jumped at the opportunity to receive Him. From that day on Lindsey had a consistent hunger to grow. Although he had many questions and plenty of issues to work through, Jesus definitely became the center of his life. Now as a college student he leads other young Christians.

If you have worked with teenagers very long, certainly you have wondered why some students accept Christ and grow like weeds, while others stagnate like dead fish?

Nothing produces more frustration than to pour your life into a student and have that student develop no more of a relationship to Jesus than he does to Napoleon Bonaparte. I wish I could give you a simple formula that would bring every student to Christ and cause them to grow to maturity. But we know the bottom line: God draws people to Himself, not us. God causes people to grow, not us.

If God isn't drawing the person, then all of our efforts will prove futile. Yet when we allow God to work, He releases us from the pressure of forcing people to grow and gives us the privilege of watching Him change lives. The Apostle Paul discusses this process in 1 Corinthians 3:6: "I planted the seed, Apollos watered it, but God made it grow." What part do we play? Certainly we can learn to plant and water effectively.

One summer my wife and I had a tomato-growing contest. Each of us had a tomato plant and a 12" by 12" patch of ground on which to grow it. Since the loser had diaper-changing duty for a month, my wife seized the moment. She grabbed a shovel, potting soil, some kind of growth food, and a pitcher of water, then proceeded to spend an hour cultivating the soil for her tomato plant. I watched with amusement, all the while taunting her with my butter pecan milkshake. Continuing to make fun, I badgered her with the question, "Why are you spending so much time on one stupid plant?" As I continued to heckle her, she smiled and responded: "We'll see."

After she finally finished, I grabbed a teaspoon, dug a hole three inches deep, stuck my tomato plant in it, covered it up, added water, and flooded it with a barrage of verbal encouragement: "Grow, baby, grow!" In only a few weeks this farmer would change no more "stinkies" for a month!

Over the next month she pampered her plant, and I ignored mine. By mid-summer I had nothing but puny, green, acorn-size tomatoes not big enough for the Keebler elves to eat. My wife had big, juicy, red, monster tomatoes the size of watermelons (a slight exaggeration, but they were big). She produced so many tomatoes that our family ate them all summer. Taking the diapers out every day was a continual reminder of my humiliating defeat.

Students respond like the tomato plants. We know we can't make them grow, but we can provide the proper atmosphere to encourage those "tender little plants." Jesus promised us that He chose us to produce fruit—fruit that lasts (John 15:16). How can we help young people grow so that the fruit will last?

A SIGNIFICANT RELATIONSHIP

Your relationship with a new believer provides the proper soil for growth. As we continue to look at the story of Jesus' encounter with the Samaritan woman, we see the priority Jesus placed on the relationship. John states it this way:

"So when the Samaritans came to him, they urged him to stay with them, and He stayed two days. And because of his words many more became believers" (John 4:40-41).

Jesus loved people! Real people! Specific individuals! Jesus had a lot to do. He had synagogue speaking engagements. The blind needed healing. The dead needed to be raised. Demons needed casting out. Yet he always had time for relationships. Jesus could have left His disciples to help the Samaritans. Instead, He took two days out of His brief life to spend with new believers, most of whom probably would never enter the door of a synagogue.

Our approach is often much different. For example, when a person accepts Christ, we may see that as the end of the process. Instead, it's the beginning. We tend to forget that when a person accepts Jesus, he becomes a part of our family forever. The privilege and responsibility of helping this person grow in Christ never ends in this lifetime.

Your relationship with a new Christian provides the proper soil for his growth.

A "FELT NEEDS" PLAN

To follow up effectively we need a good plan. A new believer's life will not change with a haphazard, casual "God loves you, so hang in there and we'll see you in heaven one day." Rather, we have the exciting privilege of helping new believers discover the wonderful resources that Jesus Christ offers to change their lives. Look at the moving and intimate way the Apostle Paul expresses this to the Colossians:

> For this reason, since the day we heard about you, we have not stopped praying for you and asking God to fill you with the knowledge of his will through all spiritual wisdom and understanding. And we pray this in order that you may live a life worthy of the Lord and may please him in every way: bearing fruit in every good work, growing in the knowledge of God, being strengthened with all power according to his glorious might so that you may have great endurance and patience, and joyfully giving thanks to the Father, who has qualified you to share in the inheritance of the saints in the kingdom of light. For he has rescued us from the dominion of dark-

ness and brought us into the kingdom of the Son he loves, in whom we have redemption, the forgiveness of sins. (Colossians 1:9-14)

To plug young people into Jesus' resources, we need to begin by dealing with their felt needs. A new Christian will state his felt needs like this: "What will my friends think? What will my parents think? Will Christ leave me if I'm bad again? What do I do now that Christ lives in me? How do I communicate with God?" On the other hand, the student needs to know some of the basic truths about walking with Christ, finding assurance of salvation, spending time with God, telling others about Christ, getting involved in the family of God, and dealing with sin.

Reach Out Youth Solutions has designed a six-session booklet *Getting Started*. It covers the most common felt needs of students who are new believers and the basic truths of growing in Christ. For information on ordering this resource, go to www.reach-out.org or call 1-800-473-9456. If you choose not to use *Getting Started*, you can use the meeting agendas that begin on page 146 instead.

In order to help a new believer get plugged in quickly to Christ's resources you will need to take several significant steps.

STEP #1: GET THE STUDENT INTO THE BIBLE IMMEDIATELY

As soon as a person accepts Christ, get him to read the Word of God immediately. When sharing Christ, always have a paperback Bible that you can give away. When you give the student the Bible, ask him to read 1 John that night. Then tell him you would like to discuss it together the next day.

STEP #2: GIVE THE STUDENT FOCUSED ATTENTION QUICKLY

When a person accepts Christ, scores of questions race through his mind: *What did I do? What happened to me when I accepted Christ? What will my friends think of me now? What will my parents think of me? Do I have to talk like a TV evangelist? Can I live a perfect life? If I blow it, will Jesus leave me?* These legitimate questions need answers quickly. And even if he doesn't get all of the answers immediately, at least he knows someone who cares and who will listen to him. During the brief few days after his decision, he will seal his relationship to Christ. That's why the sooner you meet with him, the better. Try to work it out to get together with him later the same day, or at least the day after he accepts Christ. The first week get together with him at least three times to go through three sessions in *Getting Started*. After that, schedule the meetings weekly.

To enhance that approach, invite several of this student's friends who already know the Lord to hang out with him consistently over the next several days. Engulf him in the tangible love of Christ. Invite him to join you for meals, to play ball, to study, to spend the night at your house, and to come to youth activities and to church.

STEP #3: FIND A PLACE TO MEET QUIETLY

Locate an informal place convenient for both of you, probably the same place you met to share Christ with him.

STEP #4: FOLLOW THE FORMAT SIMPLY

This simple format will help you structure the conversation for maximum influence.

- *Personal:* What is going on? Express interest in all areas of his life, not just the spiritual area.

- *Projects:* How is he doing on his assignments? Walk through the entire session with him, to make sure he is grasping and applying his new discoveries about Jesus.

- *Problems:* What are his struggles? Take plenty of time to talk about his personal life, family, and other issues significant to him. It's important to ask questions and struggle with him, even though those issues may not be part of the *Getting Started* session.

- *Prayer:* Finish the session by praying for his personal needs. After a couple of sessions, ask him to pray.

STEP #5: BRING YOUR GOAL CLEARLY INTO FOCUS

When you know your goal for each meeting, then you will have confidence about what you want to accomplish. What do you want this new believer to understand as a result of each meeting together?

Having the stated goal clearly in mind for each session of the *Getting Started* book will help both of you know exactly what you want to take away from each session.

SESSION 1:

"What Happened When I Accepted Christ?" *(Knowing Christ)*

Goal: To give the student confidence in his new relationship to Christ.

First, create an atmosphere of acceptance. Assure the student that he doesn't have to say anything to get your approval. Emphasize honesty and openness. Let the student know that you will accept him whatever he feels or thinks. When he tries to answer questions, be careful not to put words in his mouth. Allowing the student to verbalize his own thoughts will help him develop his faith.

Often the greatest hindrance for a person who wants to grow in Christ is a lack of confidence that Christ has actually come into his life. In this session you want to make sure the student understands the decision he has made. Go over the Jesus: No Equal booklet once more to help the student build confidence in the decision he has made. Work together through the following principles. Say something like, "The first step in getting to know Jesus better is to understand your relationship to him. What do you think happened to you when you accepted Jesus?"

1. What did Jesus Christ do for you when you accepted Him? Read John 1:12. (You are a child of God who has the privilege of a special relationship with Jesus Christ.)

2. What makes you different from a person who has not accepted Christ? Read 2 Corinthians 5:17. (You are a new person and can leave your old life in the past.)

3. How can you be sure that Jesus is in your life? Read 1 John 5:11-13. (You have confidence that you possess eternal life.)

4. How important are your feelings? Read John 10:27-30. (Your relationship with God is based on God's promises, not on your feelings.)

SESSION 2:

"How Do I Communicate with God?" *(Spending Time Alone with God)*

Goal: To establish the student in a daily time alone with God in the Bible and in prayer.

Young people who begin a devotional time immediately after receiving Christ grow much faster than those who do not. When a student develops the habit of spending time communicating with God, then the long-term process of his growth becomes much easier. This discipline will lead him to become "independently dependent on Jesus Christ." It lays the tracks to run on for the rest of his life.

After you review what you did in your last session, help him understand the importance of Bible study and prayer.

The recommended *Time Alone with God Notebook* will help him establish a habit of meeting with God daily. This simple approach, designed specifically for students, not only gives practical suggestions but also provides daily worksheets to walk him through this process.

Work through the following ideas together:

Say, "In the same way that your physical growth accelerates in your teenage years, your spiritual growth can speed up at the same rate. How can you grow?" Then discuss the following points.

1. Listen to Jesus. Read the Bible and let God speak to you.
  * **In what ways can the Bible help you? Read 2 Timothy 3:16-17.**
  * **What else will the Bible do in your life? Read Psalm 1:1-3.**

Begin to read the Bible daily and put into practice one insight every day.

2. Talk to Jesus. What clues about talking with God can you find in the following verses?
  * **Mark 1:35**
  * **Philippians 4:6-7**
  * **John 15:7**
  * **1 John 5:14-15**

Set aside 10 to 15 minutes to talk to God each day.

SESSION 3:

"How Do I Tell Other People?" *(Communicating to My Family and Friends)*

Goal: To tactfully, lovingly, and boldly tell friends and family about the decision to follow Christ.

What is every teenager's greatest anxiety? *What do other people think of me?*

When a teenager accepts Christ, that fear becomes even more prominent. He has made a decision that goes against the mainstream of society. Therefore, one of the student's major concerns is what friends and family will think. At the opposite end of the spectrum a young person gets really excited about his relationship to Christ and wants to tell everyone. With too much zeal and too little knowledge, he doesn't communicate tactfully. As a result he can damage his relationship with parents and friends as well as wipe out the possibility of sharing the gospel in the future.

Therefore, you need to walk him through the process of how a student can communicate with his friends and family about his new faith in a positive manner. This session helps him in two ways: (1) It strengthens him in his walk with Christ, because once he tells others positively, he doesn't have to deal with the fear of his family and friends finding out from someone else. (2) It helps him think through the best way to share Christ with his family and friends. A new believer's life will change, often dramatically. Friends and family will want to know why. If his friends don't know the real reason, they may think he is shunning them by, for example, not drinking with them as he used to. His family may wonder if he has stumbled into a weird cult. They need to know that the change is because of Christ.

In this session show him how to communicate love, not condemnation, to his family and friends. Reemphasize the significance of the ongoing, lifelong relationship with his family and the value of friendships, even if they have been the wrong kinds of friends. Help the student see how Jesus wants him to communicate in a loving manner so these people, too, can come to know Christ.

Use comments and questions like these to help him learn how to tell other people about his new faith:

What do I tell my parents? Regardless of the quality of your relationship, your parents are very important people in your life. Keep in mind the following points as you share your relationship with Christ.

Understand your parents. Not all parents will respond the same way. Whatever their response, ask Jesus to give you the ability to love them.

Don't hassle your parents.
- **Obey your parents. Read Ephesians 6:1-3.**
- **Communicate with your parents. Read Ephesians 4:15.**

- Earn your parents' trust. Read Ephesians 4:29-32.
- Recognize the needs of your parents. Read Philippians 2:3-4.

What do I tell my friends? Your friends will have one of three reactions:

- Defend. They say, "I don't need that." Read John 1:43-49 to see how one believer handled that.

- Desert. "Don't ever talk to me about God again." Read Isaiah 53:3-5 and 1 Peter 2:23 to see how Jesus handled rejection.

- Decide. "I've had a lot of questions about Jesus. Can we talk about it some time?" Read Galatians 1:10, 1 Thessalonians 1:5, John 15:12, 1 Corinthians 2:4-5, and Romans 1:16.

Verbally identify with Jesus Christ in front of your friends so He can use you to help your friends know Him.

SESSION 4:

"How Do I Get Plugged In?" (Building Relationships with Other Christians)

Goal: To help him discover new friendships in Christ.

Over the years of working with students, I have yet to find one person who has a growing relationship with Christ who has not plugged into a healthy family of believers. Without the nurture of the church, the fruit will die on the vine.

In this session our goal is to help involve this young person in a healthy, growing church. Suggest involvement in your church as one option, but not the only option. Another church might fit his relationships, family, ministry, or geographical needs better. Help him find the place where he can grow. At the same time, be sensitive to his parents' wishes—don't allow this issue to drive a wedge between the student and his parents.

Be sure to emphasize give and take in the body of Christ. Help the student see how he can receive help from others and how he can give help to others through the church. Point out that no church is perfect—all churches consist of sinners who are growing in the grace of God. Such an environment is ideal for the student's growth as a new believer. If your church is an option for him, take him with you to the youth group.

> **Help the student see how he can receive help from others and how he can give help to others through the church.**

After reviewing the session from last week, work through the following principles together:

Let others help you. Getting together with others who believe in Christ gives you a new group of friends who will help you in several ways. Read the following verses to see how that happens.
- **Ecclesiastes 4:9-16**
- **1 Thessalonians 5:11**
- **Hebrews 10:14-15**

You help others. You have something to give to other Christians. They need you. Read the following verses to discover why and how.
- **Romans 12:3-8**
- **Galatians 6:2**
- **1 John 3:16-18**

Find a church where others can help you and you can help others.

SESSION 5:

"What Happens When I Mess Up?" (Dealing with Sin)

Goal: To teach the student how to experience God's forgiveness daily.

Knowing that Christ forgives us frees us from the performance trap. That's the message we want to communicate in this session. It is one of the most difficult messages to get through because people have been programmed to think differently.

For example, when Trey asked Christ into his life he was overwhelmed with the fact that God had forgiven all his sins. We took a canoe ride to talk about this issue. He barraged me with questions. Finally he said, "Not that I have ever done this, but are you saying that even if I raped a girl, God would forgive me? Is that what you are saying?" When I answered yes, he just kept saying "WOW!" over and over. When we got to the shore, he ran up to a lifeguard he didn't even know and said, "Did you know that even if I raped a girl God would forgive me?"

The freedom of forgiveness provides the springboard for an intimate relationship with Jesus. After reviewing the session from last week, work through the following principles.

If you slap your little brother, yell at your mom, or something worse, will Jesus give up on you? Here are some answers:
- **Will Jesus give up on me? Read John 10:27-30.**
- **What happens when I sin? Read 1 John 1:5-7.**
- **How do I receive forgiveness? Read 1 John 1:9.**
- **What happens when I confess my sin? 1 Peter 2:24.**

Remember: Christians aren't perfect; they are just forgiven.

This will help the student see the incredible power of forgiveness, not only theologically, but in practical areas as well. You will want to help him learn how to experience forgiveness on a daily basis, especially applying the promise of 1 John 1:9.

SESSION 6:

"How Will My Life Change?" (Living by God's Power)

Goal: To help the student rely on God's power rather than on his own strength.

A person must decide to follow Christ daily. In fact, following Christ boils down to those moment-by-moment decisions to allow Him to control our lives. Often, students think they can pray a prayer and get Jesus the way they get new clothes. They own the clothes, but the clothes have no real affect on their lives.

By now the student is probably wondering, *Now that I know Jesus Christ, what do I have to do? What should I stop doing?* Assure him that he doesn't need to worry about that, because of the promise of John 10:10. After reviewing last week's session, work through the following principles.

Inside out. **When a person accepts Jesus Christ, the changes in his life begin on the inside, not the outside. How does the Holy Spirit change you from the inside out? Read Romans 8:9-11.**

Spiritual breathing. **Physically, you have to breathe to stay alive and healthy. You exhale and inhale. The same is true in a spiritual sense. When you breathe spiritually,**

- **You confess your sin (exhale). Read 1 John 1:9.**
- **You let the Holy Spirit control your life (inhale). Read Ephesians 5:18.**

As you learn to breathe spiritually, the Holy Spirit will change you from the inside out.

Making changes. **You may think, "I can never change." But Christ's power can change you. Read Colossians 3:1-17 to discover how He does that.**

Assure the student that God's power can change any area in his life.

Also emphasize how his decision to follow Christ affects every area of his life. Identify specific areas where he is struggling. Help him realize the importance of letting Jesus control those areas. Do this by emphasizing how Jesus changes lives from the inside out. Focus on the simple practice of spiritual breathing. Practice it together. As you go through this session he will begin to see how, through continual spiritual breathing, Christ will change his heart and then his desires and, in time, his life.

If, by the end of the six sessions, this new believer understands and applies these concepts of walking with Christ, he will be off to a great start.

A TIME INVESTMENT

You value your time, and so does your new Christian friend value his time. As you prepare to meet with him, these practical suggestions will increase the value of your time investment.

KEEP A NOTEBOOK

Keep a journal to record each appointment with students. Write down what you accomplished and what you need to cover in the next session. Record responses that seem significant, prayer requests, and questions asked. This can be the same journal that you use for campus contacts.

CALL OFTEN

During the first week, call him every day. Before your meeting, call to see if he needs any help with the session.

SPEND TIME TOGETHER

Do things with him outside of the sessions. Develop the friendship in areas besides the spiritual. Find something he enjoys and do it with him, like throwing the Frisbee or going out to eat.

BE AVAILABLE

Let him know he can call you to ask any questions or get together with you any time.

ANSWER QUESTIONS

When he asks a question, answer it specifically. Don't pretend to know the answers if you don't. But, diligently help him find the answers.Check out *Giving Away Your Faith* for answers to the seven most asked questions.

PRAY DILIGENTLY

Ask God to give him a growing hunger and thirst to know Christ more each day.

BE PATIENT

Let this person grow at God's rate, not yours. I learned this when I invested many hours working with Bobby. After he accepted Christ, he had an initial growth spurt, but then it seemed that he didn't get it after that. As the months passed I finally stopped pursuing Bobby because it seemed useless. He just wasn't growing.

Four years later, while running on the track at school, I noticed a guy with long blonde hair. He startled me when he ran up to me and said, "Hey, don't you remember me?" Then I recognized Bobby. He said, "What have you been up to?" I told him that I still do the same thing I did when he went to school: "I tell people that God loves them." He beamed and said, "Me too!" I almost fell over. Then he told me his story. In college he met a Christian bass player. Through him he had begun to grow. They formed a band, playing secular clubs and sharing the love of Christ with non-Christians. Then he looked me in the eye and said, "You know, I will never forget that day when you led me to Christ. It has changed my whole life."

HANG IN THERE! Your investment of time will pay off in time.

A 'NEW BELIEVERS' CHURCH

Following up a new Christian includes many important responsibilities, but none more important than helping him find his place in the family of God. Over the years I have seen many people come to Christ. Some have grown in Christ, and some have turned back to the world. The common thread for those who grow in Christ is that immediately they got plugged into a local church of loving Christians who cared about them. Follow-up ends and discipleship begins when a new believer becomes a part of a local church.

Follow-up ends and discipleship begins when a new believer becomes a part of a local church.

Is your church a place where a new believer can grow? If not, it would be wise to take steps to make your church as "new believer friendly" as possible, especially in the youth ministry. How do you do that?

1. *Create an entry place for new Christians.* As people grow in Christ, they tend to pick up certain phrases, cultural habits, actions, and programs that only Christians understand. But in order to enfold new Christians, we need to set aside our Christian jargon and communicate with them at their point of understanding.

At my church we create this entry point in the youth ministry with a Breakfast Club for new believers. We provide a delicious breakfast late on Saturday morning, then read what the Bible has to say about the person of Jesus Christ. The discussion centers around their questions. A source for the discussion is *Jesus: No Equal,* (the book) available from Reach Out Youth Solutions specifically for this purpose.

2. *Train your students to reach out to new believers.* Youth group kids can act cliquish. Only when the youth group opens up the circle to include others will a new Christian feel welcome in your church. Big programs, hi-tech videos, great speakers: none of that makes much difference to a kid who doesn't know anybody. If no one speaks to him or befriends him, you can be sure he won't feel welcome and he won't come back. He needs a group where he can connect. Train your students to initiate relationships with new Christians.

Train your students to initiate relationships with new Christians.

Teaching your students to reach out lovingly to new Christians starts way before this person becomes a Christian. Hopefully three people have prayed for him in a prayer triplet, and at least one person has shared Christ with him. Ask the people who know him to get with him for a Coke, to bring him to church, and to call him. Those students can take their new believer friend through *Getting Started*. Surround him with loving Christians.

3. *Encourage your students to bring him into the youth ministry and to church.* Your students will feel comfortable doing this when you train them to use the following approach.

- Ask three students who know the student to bring him (see #2 above).
- Invite him several days beforehand so he can make plans to attend.
- Offer to give him a ride, then pick him up.
- Call the night before to remind him when you will pick him up.
- Take him with you and stick with him the entire time.
- Introduce him to other people as your friend, not as "a person who just accepted Christ." When you introduce him to the entire group, don't say, "This is my friend Jim. He just accepted Christ. Stand up, Jim, and tell everybody how happy you are to know Jesus." He will feel uncomfortable enough as it is. Don't put him on the spot.
- Take him out to eat. Eating out after church or going to an activity with several other students offers one of the best ways to include him in the group.
- Talk to him about his experience at your church. Ask him, "What do you need to get out of church?" or "What do you think you can give to the church?" These questions will not only help him see the importance of church life, but also they will give you and your students insights into what new Christians need in a church.
- Invite him again next week. Gradually let him take the initiative to get to youth meetings and to church on his own. Encourage him to bring someone who needs to know Christ, especially his family and friends.

4. *Help him get into a discipleship group.* Once he has finished *Getting Started* and has begun to attend church, encourage him to become a part of the small-

group discipleship process. Get him in a group that is going through *Following Jesus.* This will ensure his ongoing growth and help him to move toward maturity.

When a young person has progressed from being totally ignorant of God, to accepting Jesus Christ, to growing in his faith, to becoming incorporated into the family of God, then you can step back and with great pleasure know that God has done a miracle and that you are seeing fruit produced—fruit that will remain. How could anyone have a higher calling or greater joy than that?

TAKING ACTION

A Personal Follow-Up Strategy

1. Describe some of the personal frustrations you've experienced in the past in trying to follow up with students.

_____

_____

_____

2. Name five key concepts that you want as part of your follow-up strategy. Back up each concept with Scripture.

Key Concept	Scripture
1._____	_____
2._____	_____
3._____	_____
4._____	_____
5._____	_____

3. Outline what you will do to help a new believer during his first 24 hours as a Christian.

_____

_____

_____

_____

_____

_____

4. Using the Personal, Projects, Problems, Prayer format and _Getting Started_, write your outline notes for each of the sessions.

Session #1: What Happened When I Accepted Christ? (Knowing Christ)

Goal:

_____

Notes:

_____

_____

_____

_____

_____

Session #2: How Do I Communicate with God? (Spending Time Alone with God)

Goal:

_____

Notes:

_____

_____

_____

_____

_____

Session #3: How Do I Tell Other People? (Communicating to Family and Friends)

Goal:

_____

Notes:

_____

_____

_____

_____

_____

Session #4: How Do I Get Plugged In? (Building Relationships with Other Christians)

Goal:

_____

Notes:

_____

_____

_____

_____

_____

Session #5: What Happens When I Mess Up? (Dealing with Sin)

Goal:

_____

Notes:

_____

_____

_____

_____

Session #6: How Will My Life Change? (Living by God's Power)

Goal:

_____

Notes:

_____

_____

_____

_____

5. With one new Christian young person in mind, design a practical plan to make your youth ministry "new believer" friendly.

Create an entry level place.

_____

_____

_____

Train your students to reach out.

_____

_____

_____

Encourage your students to invite new believers into the youth ministry and to church.

_____

_____

_____

Help new Christians get into a discipleship group.

_____

_____

_____

6. Taking into account all that you have written, what two priority actions will you take this week?

Action #1

_____

_____

Action #2

_____

_____

PART FOUR

EXPAND
THE CAMPUS
WORKFORCE

TEN

MOBILIZE STUDENTS TO REACH THEIR CAMPUS

"When does the game start?"

Shane came to summer camp. This tall, handsome junior had an enthusiastic zeal for God. He brought two of his friends to expose them to Christ. One friend wrestled with Shane on the wrestling team, and the other lived down the street from him. He cared deeply for these two guys, both of whom had been through some tough times. One friend stayed at Shane's house frequently because his dad often abused him. Shane had invested many hours in his friendship with these guys, and he wanted to know how he could lead them to Christ. In fact, that's all he wanted to talk about. When we ran together I answered question after question about walking with Christ and sharing the Lord with his friends. Shane hung onto every word.

What creates in a student a desire to see his friends come to Christ? The number one question that youth leaders ask me is, "How do I get my students motivated to share Christ?" In analyzing Shane and other motivated students, two primary characteristics stand out. First, they have a vital, daily relationship with Jesus. Second, they have a place where they live out their faith with non-believers. Instead of just going to church week after week, taking in more Bible information and having more fellowship, they take what they learn at church and apply it every week with non-Christians. They don't just go to "Christian life practice", they play the game every day.

Every year at the beginning of basketball season we would have three intense months of two and three practices a day before we ever played a game. Excitement hung in the air the first day of practice. A balance between intense competitiveness and lighthearted fun prevailed. We listened intently to the coach.

But as the days dragged on, the intensity waned. Toward the end of the three months, fights would break out among the players, and some even quit, saying it wasn't worth it. The coach would try to design new, creative drills to keep our interest, and a few times he added new plays to break the monotony. Why did we become bored? Because we were practicing for the sake of practice. We had lost sight of our goal of playing and winning games.

Many times youth groups behave similarly because they practice too much without having "games" to play. Kids get bored because they hear the same stuff over and over. We try to keep it fresh by presenting it in a different way, but it doesn't mean anything because it's just "practice." Yet the gospel demands action. By spending less time talking about it and more time doing it, our students will come alive with motivation and enthusiasm. Intuitively, students understand what the Apostle Paul understood: "The kingdom of God is not a matter of talk, but of power" (1 Corinthians 4:20).

Students must have an outlet in order to make a tangible difference in their world. In our ministries we create an environment that is either stagnant or fresh, in much the way that the Dead Sea contrasts with the Sea of Galilee. The Dead Sea is "dead" because nothing lives in it. The Sea of Galilee, by comparison, flourishes with marine life. How could two bodies of water in such close proximity be so different? Both seas have inlets, fresh streams flowing into them. But the Dead Sea has no outlet. Therefore it has no way to stay fresh and alive. Only the Sea of Galilee has an outlet flowing from it.

That illustration applies to the environment we create for our students. If they only "take in" and rarely have an outlet for their faith, then their Christian walk tends to become stagnant. Creating an outlet for Christian students means providing a place where they can flex their spiritual muscles regularly, taking on the challenge to live their faith as well as talk about it. Praying for non-Christians, standing up for their faith with their friends, seeing other students come to Christ: that's when kids come alive in their faith. Then when they come to church, they will have a hunger and desire because they know that what they learn on Sunday, they will use on Monday.

To switch from a "practice" phase to a "game" phase, you can implement these powerful principles.

CREATE THE RIGHT ENVIRONMENT

Jesus was a man with two intense concerns: (1) to do what His Father did (John 5:19-20), (2) and to "seek and to save what was lost" (Luke 19:10). Going back to the passage we have looked at so often, we see how these two concerns are inextricably woven together. After Jesus had led the Samaritan woman to salvation, the disciples asked him if he wanted something to eat. Jesus replied, "I have food to eat that you know nothing about" (John 4:32). The disciples, thinking he was holding out on them, wondered where he had obtained this food. Anticipating what they were thinking, Jesus responded,

> My food. . . is to do the will of him who sent me and to finish his work. Do you not say, "Four months more and then the harvest"? I tell you, open your eyes and look at the fields! They are ripe for harvest (John 4:34-35).

Jesus' main concerns were doing the will of His Father and saving the lost. That agenda consumed so much of his life that He called it his "food."

How do I get my students to become consumed with God and His desires to reach the lost?

If we want students to be like Jesus and to be concerned with His concerns, we need to ask: "How do I get my students to become consumed with God and His desires to reach the lost?" Creating the right environment will lead you to the answer.

ENVIRONMENT CREATOR #1—YOUR LIFE

Because of the many demands of ministry, we can easily fall into the trap of telling others how to do things, but then not do them ourselves. In all areas of the Christian life, we need to serve as the pacesetters. In no area is this more crucial than in sharing Christ. The example we set will most often determine how our students express Christ to their friends.

Ask yourself: "Do I have a lifestyle that demonstrates a desire for people to come to Christ?" I'm not talking about developing a witness-training program; I'm talking about how evangelism affects your lifestyle and the relationships around you: your neighbors, the guy that works at the gas station, the cashier at the grocery store.

That may seem removed from youth ministry, but when my young people hear about times I've shared my faith in my daily world, they see that as a model for sharing with their friends. Students will learn to share their faith by your example.

Students will learn to share their faith by your example.

ENVIRONMENT CREATOR #2 — YOUR PRAYER STRATEGY

One man has said, "Prayer is where the battle is fought. Evangelism is picking up the spoils." One major reason for the puny results of our evangelistic efforts is that we try to share Christ without prevailing prayer. Since prayer has been the prerequisite to revival throughout history, it would seem appropriate that it is a prerequisite for reaching young people today. We need a widespread prayer movement on campuses all across America.

To mobilize young people into a prayer movement, let's not start with America. Let's begin with you and your students. The spark that you ignite could become one of the contributing forces to a national awakening in America. The strategy to do this is so simple that it is profound. It takes virtually no administration, no money, and no equipment. That's different! A friend said to me, "You put into practice what you beleive every day. All the rest is just religious talk."

3 Christians Meeting Times a Week to Pray for Non-Christian Friends

The students who become part of a prayer triplet make a specific agreement to pray for and with their prayer partners. The focus is prayer. They hold each other accountable to pray. They can meet together any time—before or after school, at lunch or any other time they choose. They can even pray over the phone if they like. The prayer times need not last long, say 10 to 15 minutes.

I suggest that the prayer triplet meet for one semester. After this the commitment can be renewed if they want to continue, or they can divide up, with each person selecting two other friends who have not been involved in the prayer triplet strategy. Praying like this brings a freedom to pray like Jesus spoke about in Matthew 18:19-20:

> "Again, I tell you that if two of you on earth agree about anything you ask for, it will be done for you by my Father in heaven. For where two or three come together in my name, there am I with them" (Matthew 18:18-20).

Have them memorize these verses as God's promise to them. Then encourage them to keep notes about those they pray for and the answers they receive.

They can use a simple format like the one below during their prayer times.

1. Pray for their each other. Have them ask the Lord to help them know Jesus better and to become more like Him. Pray for their personal problems—tests, dates, lack of dates, parents, brothers and sisters, and other relationships.

2. Pray for their non-believing friends. They need to decide on three non-Christian friends they will pray for. That means each group will pray by name for nine non-believers. These prayers will focus on asking God to accomplish His purposes in the lives of these friends and to bring them to the point of receiving Christ. As a result, they will see many of their friends come to Christ. Remind them that they need to allow God to use them to answer these prayers by taking the risk to share Christ with their friends. As this strategy spreads to others in the youth group and in the schools, just imagine how the prayers for non-believers will be multiplied!

For six sessions to focus on prayer triplets with your youth group, use *Awesome Way to Pray* from Reach Out Youth Solutions.

ENVIRONMENT CREATOR #3— YOUR YOUTH ACTIVITIES

When you evaluate the activities in your youth ministry, what purposes do they serve: fun, fellowship, Bible study, prayer, leadership training, discipleship, evangelism outreach, missions? Are your activities more "inlet" or "outlet" oriented? Make a list of all of your activities, then place them in the above categories. It might surprise you.

If you implement the principles of *Jesus-Focused Youth Ministry*, then you will strike a balance here. You can order the training and resources for this strategy. You can get these by going to www.reach-out.org or by calling 1-800-473-9456.

To strike a balance between "inlet" and "outlet" activities, consider creating an overall plan based on *Jesus-Focused Youth Ministry* principles, and illustrated on page 169.

Consider the following ideas to balance "The Youth Ministry Process."[1]

- Take students with you when you talk to other students, so they can learn to share Christ with their friends. Eventually they will do this by themselves.
- Ask your leaders to take students with them when they talk to students about Christ.
- When you go on campus, spend time with your students' non-Christian friends.
- Help the students in discipleship groups make a seating chart for each class at school. Have them pray for and initiate conversation about Christ with three of those students. This approach heightens their awareness that people around them need Jesus.
- Continually challenge your students in discipleship groups to bring their non-Christian friends to youth ministry activities.
- Turn your weekly youth group meeting into an evangelistic meeting. You can schedule this as often as you think your Christian students are ready to bring their non-Christian friends.
- At those meetings, arrange the program so your students have a platform to start conversations about Christ with their friends. You can do this easily by breaking the large group into small discussion groups.
- Encourage students to share their stories publicly at these meetings. Work with them to help them communicate effectively to non-Christians.
- Utilize your discipleship students as counselors for outreach.
- Schedule outreach opportunities that focus on reaching non-Christian students.

In all of this, use balance. Make certain that you plan ministry activities so that they include significant weekly opportunities for students in evangelism and discipleship.

THE YOUTH MINISTRY PROCESS

PROCESS OF DISCIPLESHIP

EQUIPPING
- +6 Reproduction
- +5 Discipleship
- +4 Communication with God

GROUNDING
- +3 Conceptual and Behavioral Growth
- +2 Incorporation Into Body
- +1 Post Decision Evaluation

Equipping Ministry

Establishing Ministry

Ministries (arrows):
- Moving Toward Maturity 4–5
- Moving Toward Maturity 1–3
- Leadership Team
- Shepherd Ministry
- Wednesday Night Bible Study
- Evangelism Training
- Counseling Ministry Groups

NEW CREATURE

PROCESS OF EVANGELISM

HARVESTING
- -1 Repentance and Faith
- -2 DECISION to ACT
- -3 Personal Problem Recognition
- -4 Positive Attitude Toward Gospel
- -5 Grasp of Implications of Gospel

CULTIVATION/SOWING
- -6 Awareness of Fundamentals of Gospel
- -7 Positive Attitude Toward the Messenger
- -8 Initial Awareness of Supernatural Being but no knowledge of the Gospel
- -9 Awareness of Supreme Being but no Knowledge of the Gospel
- -10 No Conscious Awareness of a Supreme Being

Outreach Ministry
- Special Large Group Events

Campus Evangelism
- Campus Outreach Ministries
- Special Events

Ministries (arrows):
- Lifestyle Evangelism
- Friday Night Live
- Campus Outreach/Concert Series
- Bible Study

IMPLEMENT A PLAN THAT TRAINS STUDENTS TO REACH THEIR FRIENDS

After the Samaritan woman came to Christ, she spoke with her friends about Jesus. John wrote,

> Many of the Samaritans from that town believed in him because of the woman's testimony, "He told me everything I ever did." So when the Samaritans came to him, they urged him to stay with them, and he stayed two days (John 4:39-40).

Out of the sheer joy of knowing Jesus, the Samaritan woman shared her faith with others. But notice that Jesus stayed two days longer. Why? Obviously to lead others into a relationship with Himself. Implied in this passage is that He stayed to help the Samaritan woman and her friends grow and know how to help others in the town discover who He was.

Most young people want to communicate Christ to their friends, but they don't know how. They need encouragement and training to help them become effective in giving away their faith. You have many great tools at your disposal to help train students in evangelism.

Two resources can help you train your students in evangelism: *Taking Your Campus for Christ* prepares your students to have a strategy to radically love their friends to Christ. *Giving Away Your Faith* puts evangelism in the context of discipleship. This book is part of a five-book discipleship series called *Moving Toward Maturity*. The *Leader's Guide* will give you the tools you need to lead your students through this training. All of these books are available from Reach Out Youth Solutions by going to reach-out.org or by calling 1-800-473-9456.

Giving Away Your Faith equips students over ten weeks to communicate Christ so that students have ample opportunity to put into practice what they learn each week. The following brief synopsis of *Giving Away Your Faith* will give you an idea of what kind of specific training your students need.

CHAPTER 1 "LOST! SEEING THE NEED"

The first major barrier to students sharing Christ with their friends is getting them to believe that their friends are lost. In this sessions they make that discovery from the Bible, and then learn practical ways they can love their lost friends.

CHAPTER 2 "FROM FEAR TO FAITH: OVERCOMING FEAR"

Students' fear stands as the next major barrier that cripples their faith and prevents them from talking to their friends. In this session they discover the sources of their fear such as guilt, failure, or rejection. Then they learn how to call on the resource of faith to help them overcome their fear.

CHAPTER 3 "EXTRAORDINARY POWER: SHARING IN THE SPIRIT"

Young people discover the power of the Holy Spirit and how to make that power a personal one in their lives, especially as it relates to communicating Christ to their friends. They learn how to know when they are negatively harassing their friends in Jesus' name, and when they are positively witnessing in the Spirit.

CHAPTER 4 "A FRIEND IN NEED: MAKING FRIENDS FOR CHRIST"

Learning how to build healthy, positive relationships seems to be a struggle for all adolescents. In this session they learn how to develop and deepen friendships by showing the love of Christ to others, especially non-believers.

CHAPTER 5 "RELATE AND COMMUNICATE: STARTING A CONVERSATION"

Building the bridge from casual, everyday conversation to talking about a person's relationship to God seems to wipe many students out. They simply don't know how to start that conversation. In this session they learn how to break down conversation barriers and ask questions that build bridges to conversations about Christ.

CHAPTER 6 "MY GREAT DISCOVERY: GIVING A PERSONAL TESTIMONY"

Communicating their firsthand experience with Jesus proves difficult to most students because rarely have they thought through their own story nor have they actually prepared what they would like to say. In this session they write their story and then give it orally.

CHAPTER 7 "THE MESSAGE: PRESENTING THE TRUTH OF THE GOSPEL"

Most students want to communicate Christ to their friends but don't know how. This session helps your students communicate the truth of the gospel in a meaningful, relevant way to their friends.

CHAPTER 8 "DRAW THE NET: LEADING FRIENDS TO A DECISION"

Sometimes students will talk to their friends about Christ but never have the privilege of leading them to the Lord. They simply do not ask the deciding question. In this session they learn to ask their friends to decide for Christ.

CHAPTER 9 "HARD QUESTIONS: ANSWERING QUESTIONS NON-CHRISTIANS ASK"

This session offers an introductory course in apologetics, giving simple, practical, and biblical answers and illustrations to the seven questions that non-Christians ask the most.

CHAPTER 10 "GETTING STARTED: HELPING A NEW CHRISTIAN GROW"

Once a friend makes a decision to follow Christ, then what? In this session students learn how to help a friend grow in his new relationship to Christ, using the *Getting Started* book. This book covers all of the essential aspects needed to train your students in communicating their faith.

INITIATE A MOVEMENT OF STUDENTS TO REACH THE CAMPUS

Leading young people to Christ yourself is one thing, and training Christian students in discipleship groups to share their faith with their friends is another. But to create a movement with the goal of reaching the entire campus is quite another!

After Jesus stayed with the Samaritans for two days, John tells us: "And because of his works many more became believers" (John 4:41). Jesus created a movement! Then the friends of the Samaritan woman made an interesting comment.

> They said to the woman, "We no longer believe just because of what you said; now we have heard for ourselves, and we know that this man really is the Savior of the world" (John 4:42).

Two days with Jesus will change your life! The Samaritans had heard about Jesus from the woman, but they didn't take it to heart until they saw Jesus face to face.

Let's be honest. Most of our young people in the church are that way. They have heard it all before, and they don't get fired up about communicating their faith with anybody. Really, many of them are sick of hearing about Jesus. We can conclude that either they haven't seen the reality of Christ in others or they haven't experienced Jesus for themselves.

Taking another step toward reality, most of us must confess that we have taught them to pursue the middle-class dream of having a comfortable, upwardly mobile lifestyle with all of its high-tech toys. And, oh yes, throw Jesus in there too. That makes it all the better. No wonder our kids are apathetic and unmotivated! Most of them have never experienced the dynamic, life-changing reality of Jesus. If they had, then their attitudes, actions, habits, and goals would be radically different.

So how do you get a group of apathetic, unmotivated students in your youth group excited about following Jesus, and then about communicating Him to their friends?

In order to create a thirst for God and a desire for His plan to reach the lost, we, as youth leaders, have to take a big risk. We must let them see that they have a big God who does big things. When people reach adolescence they can no longer live on the faith of their parents, their friends, or the church. They have to either possess their own faith or reject it all together. But most students do neither. They straddle the fence. That's the reason for apathy. Individually, they have to decide if they will play on the team or quit. It's time to take a big risk and help them do that. When you do, then Jesus will come alive to them.

We must let students see that they have a big God who does big things.

The best way to move a group of students from the "Ho Hums" to "High on Jesus" is to rattle their cages! We do that by putting them into situations that force them to make decisions about what they believe. One of the most significant roles you play as a youth pastor is to make students test the reality of God.

You can rattle their cages by planning opportunities that put them in the middle of the overwhelming needs of others. Most students believe that the world revolves around them. As long as they have their clothes, their music, their friends, their toys, that's all they need. When they get out of their comfort zone and into the needs of others, they realize their own inadequacies to meet those needs. At that point, God will turn their selfish set of values on its head and cause them to call on His resources. That's when faith comes alive. The following three approaches will provide you with a variety of experiences in which you can involve your students with the bigness of God.

LOCAL ONGOING OPPORTUNITIES

To encourage these "bigness-of-God" experiences in your group, plan local monthly outreaches that place your kids nose to nose with needy people. I have found involvement in these opportunities particularly meaningful:
- Helping with Special Olympics
- Visiting retirement homes
- Visiting hospitals for terminally ill children
- Working in soup kitchens
- Staying overnight in a homeless shelter
- Painting the house of an elderly woman
- Serving Thanksgiving dinner to a poor family
- Handing out sandwiches and blankets to street people
- Helping to build a home for a homeless family

At the retirement home our group visits, I have a friend named Genell. Stricken with multiple sclerosis, Genell has been bedridden and unable to talk, walk, or control her body for 25 years. She is 50 now. Yet amazingly, she is always cheerful. Kristen, one of my students, had seen Genell several times. One day when we left, Kristen began to cry. She exclaimed, "How can I complain about my life and the problems I have when Genell has nothing and can still be happy?" God used that incident to lead Kristen out of her superficial faith and create in her a strong burden for those who are considered "the least." This happens often when you plan these kinds of opportunities for your students. They will understand that God created them to serve others, not themselves, and that their lives can make a difference.

SHORT-TERM MISSIONS TRIPS

Last summer I took groups on mission trips to Romania and Mexico. This summer we are going again. In Mexico we helped people who live in cardboard shacks build a 12' by 12' room that will serve as their home. Most of my students' bedrooms are bigger than that! In these situations the way young people view Jesus changes from seeing Him as a "blah" storybook figure into a dynamic life-changing Reality.

Students need situations that put their backs against the wall and force them to allow God to work. Naturally we depend on God only when we have to. When we don't have to, we live it out on our own. But missions trips create an atmosphere where students have to trust God to do the supernatural. For many students it is the first time in their lives their faith has been tested seriously.

> **Students need situations that put their backs against the wall and force them to allow God to work.**

For our team the first faith-builder was to see God raise $11,000 for the trip. Amy, an 11th grader, said, "This will be impossible!" She didn't want to go on the trip for that very reason. She didn't have the money and couldn't believe that God would provide it. I purposely got her signed up for the trip in order to put her in a situation that would cause her to have to trust God. As the Lord brought in her money, I enjoyed watching her change from talking about guys all the time to talking about God. She had seen a big God do a big thing for her. And we hadn't even left on the trip yet! Look into Leading Edge Trips that equip your student leaders on a cross-cultural trip. Your students will discover, experience and apply leadership qualities of Jesus on the trip. For more information on Leading Edge Trips contact us at www.reach-out.org or call 1-800-473-9456.

TOTAL CAMPUS PENETRATION

Once young people start growing in discipleship, giving their faith away to others, and meeting human needs, you, as the youth leader, need to plan a vision-stretching strategy to help them reach out to the entire campus. Here are the ingredients to remember as you think and pray about this:

1. *Begin to meet with other youth leaders in your area for prayer.* (See Chapter 3.)

2. *Mobilize your students into prayer triplets.* We hope the youth leaders you pray with can do this with their students too. Then you will have a sizeable prayer movement on the campus.

3. *Provide the opportunity for the other youth leaders in your area, especially the ones in smaller churches, to get training in Jesus-Focused Youth Ministry.* (For information on these opportunities, contact Reach Out Youth Solutions.)

4. *Bring together the churches sharing Christ on the campus.* Plan this strategy together.

5. *Network with other churches to create outreach opportunities.* Pool your resources. Assign the students being trained to bring at least three friends. Don't do promotional hype, but focus on students bringing the friends for whom they have prayed. This will work only when you have students who want to share Christ with their friends.

6. *Continue this cycle of prayer, training, and outreach for an ever-widening, constantly expanding influence for Christ on the campus.*

TAKING ACTION

A Strategy for Training Students in Evangelism

CREATE THE RIGHT ENVIRONMENT

ENVIRONMENT CREATOR #1: YOUR LIFE

On a scale of one to ten, how would you rate yourself in giving a consistent, bold witness to other adults?

(lowest) 1　　2　　3　　4　　5　　6　　7　　8　　9　　10 (highest)

What do you need to do to increase your passion and effectiveness in this area?

_____

_____

_____

On a scale of one to ten, how would you rate yourself in witnessing to young people consistently?

(lowest) 1　　2　　3　　4　　5　　6　　7　　8　　9　　10 (highest)

What do you need to do to increase your passion and effectiveness in this area?

_____

_____

_____

ENVIRONMENT CREATOR #2: YOUR PRAYER STRATEGY

Have you followed through on the strategy of praying with other youth leaders on your campus? (See Chapter 3.)

____yes ____no

If you answered no, do this step before applying anything else in this chapter.

How will you organize the prayer triplet strategy for your students?

_____

_____

_____

_____

_____

What are the first three steps you need to take to get that started?

1.

2.

3.

ENVIRONMENT CREATOR #3: YOUR YOUTH ACTIVITIES STRATEGY

Make a list of all of your activities, the specific purpose for each one, and into what categories they fit (fun, fellowship, Bible study, prayer, leadership training, discipleship, evangelism, outreach, missions).

Activity	Purpose	Category

As you evaluate it, do you have balance? What adjustments do you need to make?

_____

_____

_____

_____

To create a strategic balance in your ministry activities, fill out the following chart, not according to what you do now, but according to the adjustments you need to make. Use "The Youth Ministry Process" chart on page 182 to plan how you will balance your youth ministry.

IMPLEMENT A PLAN THAT TRAINS STUDENTS TO REACH THEIR FRIENDS

On a scale of one to ten, how would you evaluate your discipleship ministry?

(lowest) 1   2   3   4   5   6   7   8   9   10 (highest)

What steps do you need to take to have an ongoing small group discipleship ministry with your students?

_____

_____

_____

(I recommend that you go through the _Moving Toward Maturity_ series progressively so that when you train your students to share their faith, they will have built a solid foundation on which to place that strategy of evangelism.)

INITIATE A MOVEMENT OF STUDENTS TO REACH THE CAMPUS

Ongoing Local Opportunities

What ongoing local outreach opportunities do you have available to you?

_____

_____

_____

_____

_____

_____

Pick one that will stretch and challenge your students. Make sure it fits your previous strategy design. Plan a faith-stretching outreach.

Outreach Opportunity:

_____

Date:

_____

How do you foresee this strategy working on a long-term basis?

_____

_____

_____

Short-Term Missions Trips

How will taking a mission trip enhance your students' zeal for evangelism on their campus?

_____

_____

_____

_____

_____

_____

What steps do you need to take to set up a short-term mission trip?

_____

_____

_____

_____

_____

Total Campus Penetration

Outline your vision for seeing God move in a way that would penetrate the entire campus. (Include prayer, training, and outreach.)

_____

_____

_____

_____

_____

_____

_____

_____

_____

_____

_____

NOTES

1. The scale on the two charts used in this chapter is borrowed from a chart entitled "The Spiritual Decision Process" in What's Gone Wrong with the Harvest? by James S. Engel and H. Wilbert Norton (Grand Rapids, Mich.: Zondervan, 1975), 45.

THE YOUTH MINISTRY PROCESS

PROCESS OF DISCIPLESHIP					
	EQUIPPING	+6	Reproduction	Equipping Ministry	
		+5	Discipleship		
		+4	Communication with God		
	GROUNDING	+3	Conceptual and Behavioral Growth	Establishing Ministry	
		+2	Incorporation Into Body		
		+1	Post Decision Evaluation		

NEW CREATURE

PROCESS OF EVANGELISM					
	HARVESTING	-1	Repentance and Faith	Outreach Ministry	
		-2	DECISION to ACT		
		-3	Personal Problem Recognition		
		-4	Positive Attitude Toward Gospel		
		-5	Grasp of Implications of Gospel		
	CULTIVATION/SOWING	-6	Awareness of Fundamentals of Gospel	Campus Evangelism	
		-7	Positive Attitude Toward the Messenger		
		-8	Initial Awareness of Supernatural Being but no knowledge of the Gospel		
		-9	Awareness of Supreme Being but no Knowledge of the Gospel		
		-10	No Conscious Awareness of a Supreme Being		

ELEVEN

MULTIPLY LEADERS FOR THE CAMPUS

"So many students and so little of me."

This chapter focuses on raising up leaders for campus ministry. To do that with excellence, you will need to recruit and equip your Leadership Team. You can discover how the Leadership Team fits into your ministry by going through *Jesus-Focused Youth Ministry*. To raise up the team of adult volunteers who will multiply your ministry, use *Building Leaders for Jesus-Focused Youth Ministry*.

Sitting in the parking lot of Wal-Mart for three hours was not normally what I did on Friday afternoon. But I parked there on this particular day to cry out to God about how unfair life is. I searched desperately for an answer to my frustration.

Life had overwhelmed me. In addition to an already booked forty-hour week, I had three meetings and a worship service to plan. Three new Christians needed follow-up. I had promised to get together with two non-Christian students. Now Friday afternoon had come and gone and I had done none of it. In addition, I had spent zero time with my family.

The final straw came when my daughter crossed me. Now I was crying out to God. "How could you give me so many needs and opportunities but not give me the time and energy to meet them? I can't even meet the everyday needs in my little circle of influence, much less all of the other ones out there. And my family..." I felt so overwhelmed, so inadequate, so small.

Certainly Jesus could have felt the same way as He looked out on the crowds of people with multiple needs (Matthew 9:36). If He had let happen to him what happened to me, He would have said, "Quick, let's get over there right now before it's too late. That blind man could get run over by a Mack chariot and never know about me." Thankfully Jesus had His Father's perspective, which led Him to say, "The harvest is plentiful but the workers are few. Ask the Lord of the harvest, therefore, to send out workers into his harvest field" (Matthew 9:37). Even with the immensity of the task, I sense a lack of anxiety in His voice. When Jesus says, "Ask the Lord of the harvest", He reveals the secret for solving my particular mess. God is in control!

After my attitude adjustment, I needed a vision adjustment. I needed a refresher course in Jesus' view of ministry, as opposed to my view. Somehow, I had fallen into the trap of thinking that if I didn't reach every student for Christ, I could not receive the coveted "Well Done, Good And Faithful Servant Award". My goal of reaching students with the message of Christ got misdirected because I thought I had to do everything myself.

The first practical paradigm shift came when I began to see that instead of trying to do all of the ministry myself, I needed to train "the laborers" to go out into the harvest field with me. The needs of the campus are too great to ever think about meeting those needs by ourselves. We must multiply ourselves in the lives of others, in order to share the task. Interestingly, when we study the New Testament, we see that no one ever operates as "The Lone Ranger" in ministry. In fact, it is always a team effort.

> **The needs of the campus are too great to ever think about meeting those needs by ourselves.**

The second practical paradigm shift developed when I began to broaden my vision. As frustrated as I felt about what I couldn't get done, I realized that I really had not seen the whole picture. Matthew 9:35 helped me see that Jesus went through "all the towns and villages." He had a plan for each one of those places. Not only that, but also He "saw the crowds." In John 4, the passage we have thoroughly examined, Jesus saw the fields white for harvest (v. 36).

I began to realize that I had limited my vision for what Jesus wanted to do on the campus. I saw one campus. He saw all of the campuses.

For the first time I considered the question, "How do I establish a viable ministry on every campus in my section of the city?" Then I began to dream how I could develop "Campus Teams"—adults trained as a ministry team to do on other campuses what I had done on mine. I envisioned college students and interns leading these teams, with parents, teachers, and lay workers joining them to produce an all-out assault on the campus for the cause of Christ. My frustration turned to sheer excitement!

Then the third paradigm shift clicked in when I ran Matthew 9:35 through my mind again. I read "teaching...preaching the good news of the kingdom and healing every disease and sickness." Enrolling in a quick refresher course on Jesus' ministry, I began to see applications I had never seen before. At the initial stage of His ministry, Jesus told the synagogue congregation what He had come to do. In Luke 4:18-19, quoting Isaiah 61:1, He set forth His mission:

> The Spirit of the Lord is on me, because he has anointed me to preach good news to the poor. He has sent me to proclaim freedom for the prisoners and recovery of sight for the blind, to release the oppressed, to proclaim the year of the Lord's favor (Luke 4:8-19).

Jesus described for His audience what they would see Him doing:

(1) preaching the good news, (2) healing the sick, and (3) delivering the oppressed. Flip through the pages of the Gospels, and you will see that what Jesus said He would do that day, He did.

But Jesus didn't stop there. He taught His disciples to do exactly what He had done. When I read Mark 6:12-13, I understood what Jesus had trained His disciples to do. "They went out and preached that people should repent. They drove out many demons and anointed many sick people with oil and healed them." They did exactly what they had seen Him doing. The disciples (1) preached the good news, (2) healed the sick, and (3) delivered people from demon oppression.

Then the Lord showed me the real kicker. I saw for the first time the practical reality of the phenomenal promise of John 14:12.

> I tell you the truth, anyone who has faith in me will do what I have been doing. He will do even greater things than these, because I am going to the Father.

I looked at that word "anyone". Who is that? Then it hit me. That includes me! And not only me, but also all those I train for ministry. The Jesus who demonstrated His presence and power in preaching the Good News, healing the sick, and delivering the oppressed is the same Jesus who lives in me to carry out those same ministry objectives. But even greater, He lives in my team of leaders as well and will just as powerfully carry out His ministry through them. And His promise includes you too. You can have the very same ministry that Jesus had!

It became very clear to me that in the youth culture of today each of those ministries of Jesus need to be modeled in our youth ministries. We need to preach the Good News because young people desperately need a relationship with Christ. We must heal the sick because today's students come from such dysfunctional backgrounds that they desperately need emotional healing from the deep wounds inflicted on them, and sometimes they need physical healing. We must deliver the oppressed because of the strongholds Satan has on young people who are addicted to drugs, alcohol, sex, Internet pornography, and a host of other life-destroying habits. The practical reality of the world of adolescence forces us to practice the ministry of Jesus.

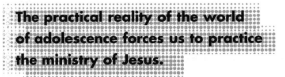

The practical reality of the world of adolescence forces us to practice the ministry of Jesus.

It turned out to be quite an afternoon in the parking lot. After that experience, I began to consider how I could work out in my ministry the new vision the Lord had given me. As I further considered how Jesus trained His leaders, the fog began to lift, and I saw the practical pattern of how to incorporate these new paradigm shifts to raise up skilled laborers for the harvest.

MODEL—"I DO IT!"

If you want to frustrate a potential leader, ask him to do something that he has never seen or done before. Jesus never did that to His disciples. He never asked them to do anything that He wasn't willing to do Himself first. He put a high priority on setting the example.

A series of significant decisions confronted me as I pondered my role as a pacesetter. How did I need to set the pace? I had already crossed the bridge of setting the example in my personal walk with the Lord. That held the highest priority for me. And I had crossed the bridge of actually doing campus ministry myself. But I had two decisions to make.

First, how would I set the pace in establishing ministries on other campuses? I decided that I would use my campus as a training ground to equip other leaders, then I would help them take the first few steps in getting established on a new campus. I knew the new campus needed to be their ministry, not mine.

Second, how would I carry out the threefold ministry of Jesus myself? In prayer I determined that no matter how others viewed me, I needed to step out on the promise of John 14:12 and to look aggressively for opportunities to express Jesus' ministry of preaching, healing, and delivering.

As that began to work itself out, I found that not only did I have new opportunities for ministry, but I also had new power in my ministry. As I "preached the Good News" in one-on-one evangelism and in speaking opportunities, many more young people responded with a refreshing excitement about Jesus.

As I got rid of my hang-ups about healing the sick, people began to call me asking me to pray for them about their illnesses. I witnessed the Lord's healing hand on cancer in my own family and in other people as well. One leadership couple experienced healing from infertility; another leader suffering from toxic shock syndrome was healed. I enjoyed a fresh, new satisfaction of ministry as opportunities emerged to pray for young people who needed emotional healing. Exhilaration describes the experience of watching them release resentment and bitterness toward divorced parents, forgive fathers for sexual abuse, and allow the hurts of neglect to be covered by the balm of God's love.

Delivering the oppressed opened up a whole new realm to me. I began to learn about spiritual warfare, the demonic, and the occult. Somehow I had my head in the sand before this time. As soon as I began to pray that the Lord would use me to carry out His ministry every day, I spoke at a white water rafting camp for 600 mostly non-Christian students. On the first day I met a young man I'll call Don. He was a smoker and a funky dresser, but that wasn't unusual for this group. I liked him. We talked several times. Don listened to my talks. On the night I offered the opportunity, he received Christ. The next afternoon the youth pastor, in a panic, came to get me. Don was exhibiting some weird behavior.

As the youth pastor and I talked to Don, he told me that he listened for hours to openly satanic heavy metal groups and that he often used a Quija board. He played a satanic game every week. Ritual sex and drugs were part of his background. His mom had a library of books on death and the occult. It didn't take a spiritual giant to recognize that Satan had established a number of strongholds in Don's life. It became apparent that a demonic influence was present when this very nice, sweet-natured young man's eyes suddenly glazed over and his voice became a guttural growl.

The youth pastor and I took some rather simple steps. (1) We invited the presence of God into that room through praise. (2) We had Don confess all of his sin, the key factor that loosened Satan's grip on his life. (3) We prayed that we would overcome Satan "by the blood of the Lamb and the word of [our] testimony" (Revelation 12:11). Through a series of prayers and confrontations, the demons released their grip on various areas of Don's life. He walked out of that room totally free.

Quite frankly, I'm amazed at how many kids have been caught in Satan's grasp and need to be set free. Who will "deliver the oppressed" unless those of us in youth ministry do it? What an awesome privilege to model Jesus' ministry through the Spirit living in me to kids and other leaders. And you can do that same ministry!

MOTIVATE—"I DO IT, AND THEY ARE WITH ME."

Once I began to set the pace, I wanted to bring others into the process with me. Jesus did that. Over and over we read that the disciples were "with him" or that He was "with them." He made his disciples a part of the training process. On one occasion Jesus and the disciples got into an overwhelming situation (humanly speaking). They had more than 5,000 people to feed. Foreseeing what was about to happen, the disciples tried to cut this potentially difficult experience off at the pass.

"It was late in the day, so his disciples came to him. 'This is a remote place,' they said, 'and it's already very late. Send the people away so they can go to the surrounding countryside and villages and buy themselves something to eat"' (Mark 6:35-36).

In other words, "Hey, Jesus, let's not get ourselves in a bind here. We need to act now before it's too late." Jesus wasn't so quick to let them off the hook. "But he answered, 'You give them something to eat' "(v. 37). No longer spectators, the disciples followed Jesus' instruction to collect the food they had (five loaves and two fishes) and to hand it out. You can imagine the disciples' astonishment watching the food multiply as it passed from their hands to the hands of the people in front of them! How amazed they must have been when they collected twelve extra baskets of food. How motivated do you think they were after that?

That same kind of action-oriented participation in youth ministry motivates people. Teachers will eagerly go beyond spending one boring hour on Sunday mornings and they will relish involvement in the process of changing kids' lives.

I realized one day that watching someone's example was how I learned youth ministry. My Young Life leader in college, Mal McSwain, met with a group of us every Sunday afternoon to teach us how to work with teenagers, and then took several of us to the campus every week. We went with him, watching, observing, meeting kids, getting in on ministry experiences, seeing kids come to Christ.

As I thought about what Mal had done with me, it became clear to me that people learn more by seeing and doing than by sitting and hearing. As I've taken people with me, I've found that, although watching helped the learning process, they wanted in on the action.

To go from "watching" to "doing," follow a process that "lets the string out a little at a time."

1. *Take another leader with you to observe.* Encourage him to keep a notebook like you keep and to write in it what he sees and learns in every ministry opportunity.

2. *Give your leader serving tasks.* At the beginning have him do tasks that develop a servant's attitude. Give him jobs such as picking up a book for the person you are going to see or driving the car to the appointment.

3. *Ask your leader's advice.* When you finish an appointment, ask him what he

observed. Then ask, "What would you do next with this person?"

4. *Get your leader to help you in simple ministry tasks.* Tell him beforehand what you want him to do. For example, ask him to carry the conversation for the first five minutes of the appointment, pray at the end of the appointment, or meet three new people on campus and tell you their names.

5. *Give your leader more ministry responsibility.* Again let him know beforehand what you will ask of him. When you are sharing Christ with someone, ask him to give his testimony, share the gospel, or lead in the prayer to receive Christ. In other ministry opportunities let him pray for a pregnant teenager's family or initiate the conversation with a young person whose parents are getting divorced.

6. *Let your leader carry every part of the ministry opportunity.* Ask him to carry the entire conversation on an evangelistic appointment. When a teenager runs away, let him take care of the situation while you tag along for support. Let him pray for healing when a teenager is sick. Bail him out if necessary. But if he stumbles, let him see if he can get the situation resolved. Come to the rescue very slowly. Let him carry the full weight of the ministry responsibility.

7. *Follow up with your leader after every encounter.* Ask questions and have him make observations in his journal. What happened? What went well? What could we have done better? Be honest in your evaluation, but always give affirmation and encouragement.

When you motivate leaders by letting them in on the action, they will want to get even more involved on campus.

MOBILIZE—"THEY DO IT, AND I AM WITH THEM."

After Jesus demonstrated for the disciples what to do and let them do it with Him, then He sent them out on their own. Jesus let the rope out even more.

In Luke 9, notice how Jesus set this up. First, He didn't send them out alone; they went as a team (v. 1). Then He extended his power and authority to them (v. 1). Without this they would have gotten clobbered. Notice what they had power and authority to do: (1) to preach the kingdom of God, (2) to cure diseases, and (3) to drive out all demons. Then Jesus gave them specific, practical instructions on how to conduct themselves as they carried out His ministry. Then He sent them out to do what He had given them the power and authority to do. And that's exactly what they did!

This "experiment" went so well that Jesus gathered 72 others and sent them out with the same instructions (Luke 10:1-24). When they returned and told Jesus that "even the demons submit to us in your name" (v. 17), He replied, "I saw Satan fall like lightning from heaven" (v. 18). What an incredible testimony of how Christ can mobilize His followers with His power and authority to impact not only what goes on in the physical world but also in the spiritual realm. So how do we mobilize our leaders that way? One thing is certain: When we mobilize our leaders as Jesus did, they will respond with enthusiasm.

> **One thing is certain: When we mobilize our leaders as Jesus did, they will respond with enthusiasm.**

Anton, a young man from Puerto Rico by way of New York, had worked with me for quite a while. I had trained him in ministry through our Leadership Team. He had gone with me on numerous ministry opportunities, and I had recently sent him out on his own to see what would happen.

"You won't believe it!" Anton shouted as he walked into my office. "You just won't believe it!" Then he went on to tell me that as he was driving home with his friend Shane from a ball game, Shane asked Christ to come into his life. Anton was beside himself. For months he had played basketball and video games, spent lots of money on gas, and spent hours in prayer, all so Shane could come to know Christ. Anton had done it without any involvement on my part.

He had made the wonderful discovery that God could use him to change another person's life. His confidence soared. Our conversations began to change from "Can you help me with this person?" to "I'm going to share Christ with Michael today." After that Anton started a ministry at a shelter for juvenile delinquents. Now he is a youth pastor.

How do we get people like Anton mobilized to do ministry on their own? These suggestions will help us move in that direction.

1. Send your leaders out in teams. Not only does this follow the New Testament model, but also it offers protection, encouragement, help, and prayer support. Give each team a campus or an area of ministry for which they take total responsibility.

2. Officially release God's authority to your leaders. Schedule a service at your church to lay hands on these teams, commissioning them in their ministry. This will not only release the power of Christ in them for ministry, it will also place the full authority of the church behind them.

3. Remind your leaders of their mission often. As you meet with them, always keep the vision in front of them: to carry out the ministry of Jesus on the campus.

4. Give your leaders initial instructions. Conduct a retreat for them as the school year begins. Spend the weekend working through their plans and activities for the year.

5. Give your leaders their own specific responsibilities. Put each one's responsibility in writing, explaining exactly what you expect. For example, while in college, after I had worked in one youth ministry for a year, I was assigned a high school campus. The leader took me there, introduced me to the principal, and gave me a schedule and a list of responsibilities. I knew exactly what I was expected to do.

6. Make certain that your leaders follow through. As you send out your leaders, the way to ensure that they go is to give them reasonable deadlines. For example, when my leader sent me to the campus, he told me to have lunch on the campus every Thursday and to attend the football game every Friday. It was not too difficult for him to check and see if I had followed through on my responsibility.

7. Check with your leaders along the way. As you work with your campus ministers, you will need to check with them frequently. Do whatever is needed to make them successful. Encourage them. Help them. Go with them. Pray with them. For example, when my campus leader saw that I was struggling to follow through on my visits to the principal and coaches, he went with me. Together we accomplished the goal. It worked because he stuck with me.

8. Meet with your leaders each week for continued training. Build them into your Leadership Team. You will find that this meeting is something they look forward to because it provides support. There they can share their victories and their failures and find encouragement in both. For example, when my leader trained me in college, we had "Leadership" every Sunday afternoon. I looked forward to that time; it was the highlight of my week.

9. *Keep your leaders going.* As you train your leaders, wisely cut down on the amount of time you spend in active ministry with kids in order to spend more time with your leaders. Give them more and more of the responsibility for the students. Keep your personal campus ministry going. Don't make the mistake of abandoning it. Your sacrificial investment will motivate them and keep them going while multiplying your ministry.

MULTIPLY — "THEY DO IT AND I AM IN THE BACKGROUND TO ENCOURAGE"

After the Resurrection, the Holy Spirit came at Pentecost. The disciples were given the Spirit of Jesus to continue what Jesus had started. That's what Jesus said would happen:

> You will receive power when the Holy Spirit comes on you; and you will be my witnesses in Jerusalem, and in all Judea and Samaria, and to the ends of the earth (Acts 1:8).

Then all of those Spirit-filled people scattered over the face of the earth. As we turn the pages of Acts and Paul's letters, we observe that the disciples did exactly what Jesus had done and what they had been trained to do: they taught, they healed, and they delivered from demons, only they did it without Jesus' physical presence. They operated by the Spirit.

That incredible legacy has continued down through the centuries so that now the ministry of Jesus has multiplied across the face of the earth. In AD 100 there was one believer for every 360 people on earth. Now there is one believer for every 7.1 people on earth.[1] We are moving rapidly to the climax of history. Before too much longer God's objective will be realized: that the blood that purchased men for Him will draw individuals from "every tribe and language and people and nation" (Revelation 5:9).

What an amazing opportunity and privilege we have to participate in God's move-ment, to raise up other leaders to participate in that movement, and to take the gospel to what could very well be the generation that fulfills the Great Commission and paves the way for Jesus' return!

> **This could very well be the generation that paves the way for Jesus' return!**

Multiplication speeds God's process along. And you can speed the multiplication process by following these guidelines.

1. *Train your leaders through a Leadership Team.* Use *Building Leaders for Jesus-Focused Youth Ministry* first, then take them through the training in this book. By that time you will have completed the first three phases with them (model, motivate, and mobilize). Note that often the best people to involve in campus ministry are college students. They can give large amounts of time to building relationships with students.

2. *Make a list of the campuses in your area, both middle school and high school.* Pray over them, asking the Lord where He wants you to send the people you train.

3. *Out of your prayers for the campus, select the one campus (or more) that you will target next.*

4. *Assign a team to that campus.* Put into practice each of the chapters of this book. As more teams receive training, assign them to other campuses.

5. *Get your leaders started by going with them yourself.* Get them to the point where they have developed a positive relationship with the principal and know their way around the school.

6. *Target one campus after another until every campus has a vital ministry.* Realize that all of this does not have to come from the resources of your church. Other church-es and youth organizations may already have established campus ministries. Network together with them for a powerful, united youth ministry coalition in your community.

7. *Consider the possibility of utilizing interns in this process.* Students considering youth ministry as a possible vocation make excellent interns. Place interns in a lead-ership team. Place them under a veteran leader. Assign each of them to a campus. That campus will become his youth ministry where he will build relationships, evan-

gelize, disciple, and mobilize Christian students to reach their friends for Christ. In time he will train other leaders to go to other campuses.

Would my youth leader in college, Mal McSwain, who took all of these steps with me, have ever imagined that my pitiful efforts at the time would have led to a life committed to multiplying youth ministries around the world? No way! But his faithfulness raised up numerous leaders like me. If you are faithful to model, motivate, and mobilize your leaders, in due time God will multiply your efforts!

TAKING ACTION

A Strategy for Training Campus Ministry Leaders

1. Evaluate your current campus ministry training.

Through how many weeks of training have you taken your Leadership Team?

     0   6   12   18   24   30   36

(If you have not started a Leadership Team, do so before following the other instructions in this book for training your campus leaders.)

What steps have you taken to *model* campus ministry?

_____

_____

_____

What steps have you taken to *motivate* campus leaders?

_____

_____

_____

What steps have you taken to *mobilize* campus leaders?

_____

_____

_____

What *multiplying* results have you seen from any of the above?

_____

_____

_____

2. Implement campus ministry training.

MODEL

To *model* campus ministry consistently, fill out these accountability questions now, then write them in your journal to use weekly. They will help you to stay sharp in modeling campus ministry.

Was I on campus during my "designated hours" this week?

_____

With how many non-Christians have I spent time this week?

_____

With how many new believers have I spent time this week?

_____

In what ways did I model the ministry of Jesus (preaching, healing, delivering) this week?

_____

_____

_____

How much time have I spent training my leaders this week?

_____

MOTIVATE

To *motivate* potential campus leaders, what can you do to cut them in on the action with you?

Person   Action

_____   _____

_____   _____

_____   _____

_____   _____

_____   _____

MOBILIZE

To *mobilize* leaders for their own campus ministry, what do you need to do to get them ready for their own campus responsibilities?

Person   Responsibility   Preparation

_____   _____   _____

_____   _____   _____

_____   _____   _____

_____   _____   _____

_____   _____   _____

How will you check with your campus leaders to keep them accountable to go and keep going to the campus?

_____

_____

_____

What will you do to have ongoing, weekly training for your campus leaders?

_____

_____

_____

MULTIPLY

What prayerful plan will set in motion a ministry to every campus in your area?

_____

_____

_____

_____

Fill in the specific strategy here:

Campus	Campus Team	Date to Begin	Steps to Get Ready

From this campus strategy, what three actions do you need to take during the next month?

1.

2.

3.

NOTES

1. Statistics from the Lausanne Committee Statistical Task Force.

TWELVE

UNDERSTAND THE LEGAL ASPECTS OF THE CAMPUS

"I have my rights. . .you're wrong!"

Kevin slowly opened the letter. The principal at the school where he ate lunch with students had sent it to him.

> Dear Kevin,
> Because of restrictions presented to us by the law, specifically those trelating to separation of church and state, we must ask you to remain off the campus during school hours. We are sorry for this difficult situation, but we simply have no choice.
>
>
>
> Sincerely,
> James Frost
> Principal
>
>

Kevin couldn't believe what he read, much less understand why. Immediately he called the principal to see if he had done anything wrong to provoke this step. The principal apologized for having to write the letter and acknowledged that Kevin had been a positive influence on the students and had always conducted himself appropriately. Nevertheless, the principal told Kevin that the law prohibited him from coming on the campus during school hours for "religious purposes."

People who minister to students on public school campuses frequently hear that the law prohibits them from ministering on the public school campus. Is that right? Is it true? What can we do on the campus? What are the limits? Youth ministers and

*Chapter Twelve was researched and the outline prepared by Marshall Albritton, an attorney who practices law in Nashville, Tennessee. The authors wish to express their gratitude to Marshall for this contribution.

other Christian workers increasingly find themselves having to deal with these kinds of issues. What does the law allow? Was the principal who wrote my friend correct? How do we address some of the legal issues involving student ministries as they relate to public schools? This chapter provides those of us who minister on campus with a basic understanding of the laws that apply to our activities.[1] As we look into these issues, let's remind ourselves again that getting on the campus is not about rights but about submission and service.

THE FIRST AMENDMENT AND RELIGION IN THE PUBLIC SCHOOLS

Most of the legal issues regarding religion in the public schools are decided by looking to the First Amendment of the United States Constitution.[2] The First Amendment reads as follows:

> Congress shall make no law respecting an establishment of religion, or prohibiting the free exercise thereof; or abridging the freedom of speech, or of the press; or of the right of the people peaceably to assemble, and to petition the government for a redress of grievances.

This amendment contains two provisions relating to religion. One clause forbids the state from prohibiting others from exercising their religion. It is called the *free exercise clause*. The other clause prohibits the state from establishing a religion. It is called the *establishment clause*. The establishment clause has been the chief vehicle through which the courts have restricted religious practices in the public schools. When does the state make a law regarding the establishment of religion? The United States Supreme Court has used a three-pronged test to determine whether a statute or policy has the effect of establishing a religion.

1.The statute must have a secular legislative purpose;

2.That statute's principal or primary effect must be one that neither advances nor inhibits religion; and

3.The statute must not foster an excessive government entanglement with religion. (Lemon v. Kurtzman, 403 U.S. 602 [1971]).[3]

The test developed in the Lemon v. Kurtzman case has been dubbed the Lemon test.

In some of the more well-known cases, the Supreme Court has specifically held that certain practices are prohibited by the First Amendment. These practices include on-premises religious training,[4] required recitation of prayer,[5] required daily Bible reading before class,[6] the mandatory posting of the Ten Commandments,[7] and a daily moment of silence to be used expressly for prayer.[8] The Supreme Court determined that all of these practices were unconstitutional establishments of religion.

Of these cases, *McCollum v. Board of Education* has the most direct application to youth workers who seek to minister to students on the public school campus. In that case the Supreme Court held that religious instruction could not be held on public school premises as a part of the school program, even though the instruction was conducted by personnel not associated with the public school.[9]

In *Zorach v. Clauson*, however, the court held that a similar program which was conducted off school premises was permissible. The difference in these cases was that in *McCollum* the program presented students with a symbol of the union of church and state. The courts do not want students to perceive that the school is endorsing a particular religion. There is also a concern that students not be compelled, coerced, or subtly pressured to engage in religious activities.[10]

The lower federal courts and state courts have taken the opinions of the Supreme Court and applied them in a number of situations too numerous to examine here. School administrators regularly appeal to those court decisions to support their decisions with respect to access to the school campus by student ministries.

In addition to the concerns regarding religion, the courts have also generally recognized that public school officials have an interest in maintaining discipline and avoiding a disruption of the educational process. Therefore, no citizens have an unqualified right to enter the public school campus without the permission of school officials. An informal survey of school officials and youth workers by the author has revealed that school administrators have become increasingly reluctant to allow outside parties to enter the campus without an invitation. Unless there is provable wrongdoing on the part of the officials, this practice is permissible. Such restrictions make sense in light of the number of dangerous persons and influences who seek access to public school students.

As a result of knowing this, youth leaders can maximize the opportunity to get on the public school campus by having a relationship with the administration who invites them to come to the campus. The degree of access usually depends on the attitude and temperament of the school administrative personnel and the existence of any groups who might put pressure on otherwise friendly administrators to deny access. Effective youth leaders know the utmost importance of building good relationships with school administrative personnel before making unannounced visits to see students at the local campus. A solid relationship of submission and service with sympathetic administrators will produce greater access to students than is often possible under current laws.

> **Youth leaders can maximize the opportunities they have to get on the public school campus by submission and service to the school administration.**

RIGHTS OF STUDENTS AND TEACHERS

While current First Amendment interpretation prohibits public schools from observing certain religious practices, and while youth leaders may have only restricted access to the public high schools during school hours, youth leaders should know that the Constitution protects the rights of students in the public schools.

In *Tinker v. Des Moines Independent Community School District 10*, the Supreme Court held that the First Amendment protected the right of public school students to wear armbands during school hours in protest of the Vietnam War. The Court held that wearing armbands was a form of free expression closely akin to pure speech, which was protected by the First Amendment. The Court held that students have a right under the First Amendment to express their views unless that expression (1) materially and substantially interferes with the requirements of appropriate discipline in the operation of the school; or (2) invades or collides with the rights of others. [11]

The same rules apply to students who wish to express their religious views on the public school campus. Students also have the right under the First Amendment to freely associate with others who are likeminded. [12]

Some youth leaders have found that occasionally a hostile administrator may attempt to intimidate Christian students from expressing their views or from sharing their faith on the campus. The United States Constitution protects students in such situations, and both the students and the administration should be informed of this fact. Youth leaders can conclude, then, that the Constitution protects the student who wishes to share his faith and disciple others. In addition, youth leaders need to inform their students regarding their constitutional rights without engendering a rebellious spirit on their part.

The Constitution protects the student who wishes to share his faith and disciple others.

Teachers also have a right to express their views under the First Amendment. As the Supreme Court stated in Tinker, "It can hardly be argued that either students or teachers shed their constitutional rights. . .at the schoolhouse gate."[13] Therefore, the test set forth in Tinker has also been applied to teachers.'[14]

Teachers are entitled to express their views under First Amendment protection, but the courts do not give as much latitude to such expression because of a concern that students may interpret that the school approves or officially sanctions the teachers' views. Also, teachers are not permitted to use the classroom to indoctrinate students.[15] Youth leaders can therefore serve teachers by helping them develop strategies that will permit them to express their views without violating the prohibition on indoctrination.

Youth leaders can serve teachers by helping them develop strategies for their classrooms.

An excellent group that supports teachers in this regard is The Christian Education Association International, P.O. Box 41300, Pasadena CA, 91114, www.ceai.org (888) 798-1124.

THE EQUAL ACCESS ACT

In addition to the provisions of the First Amendment the Equal Access Act also protects the rights of students.[16] The United States Congress passed the Equal Access

Act in response to reports of widespread discrimination against religious speech in the public schools and court decisions that prohibited students from meeting voluntarily on school premises during non-instructional time for prayer and fellowship.[17]

Public schools have a "limited open forum" that allows non-curriculum-related student groups to meet on the school premises outside of class time. The Equal Access Act provides students that right to meet for religious, political, philosophical, or other purposes.

Often a limited open forum is created when schools permit students to join various student groups or clubs that meet on school premises. If groups such as the chess club and the scuba club are allowed to meet, the Equal Access Act states that the school must also allow students who wish to meet for religious purposes to do so.

In *Board of Education of Westside Community Schools v. Mergens,*[18] the Supreme Court held that the officials at Westside High School violated the Equal Access Act by refusing to allow a high school student to form a Christian club that would meet for Bible study and fellowship. This club would have had the same privileges and would have operated on the same terms and conditions as the other clubs at Westside High School. In that case, the Supreme Court also held that the Equal Access Act did not violate the establishment clause of the First Amendment. The court applied the three-pronged *Lemon* test in its analysis. The court noted that the Act had a secular legislative purpose. The Act on its face granted equal access to both secular (political and philosophical) and religious speech. The Act did not have the primary effect of advancing religion.

The Equal Access Act did not require that the school endorse religious speech, but it required that the school simply permit students to exercise free speech on a nondiscriminatory basis, that is, religious speech was treated the same as nonreligious (political and philosophical) speech. The Act also limited participation by school officials at the student religious group meetings, thereby avoiding the problems of students' emulation of teachers as role models.

Also, the Act did not foster an excessive entanglement between the school and religion. The Act prohibited faculty members from participating in—and nonschool persons from directing, controlling, or regularly attending—the meetings. The court noted that a denial of equal access might well create greater entanglement problems in the form of invasive monitoring to prevent religious speech that might occur at the meetings.

The Equal Access Act and the Mergens decision are important developments regarding the rights of public school students. However, the Equal Access Act does not provide any additional rights with respect to youth leaders. In this respect, the Act has been misunderstood by many youth workers. The import of the Act is to give equal access to students, not to third parties. In fact, the Equal Access Act specifically states that meetings protected by the Act must be "student-initiated" and that "nonschool persons may not direct, conduct, control, or regularly attend such meetings." The Act does not define what constitutes directing, conducting, controlling, or regularly attending a meeting. Regardless, youth workers should be aware that school officials may attempt to use the terms of the Act itself to exclude their attendance at student-initiated Bible clubs and prayer group meetings and to prevent them from coming on the campus for any other reasons.

Are there any circumstances in which a youth worker would have a legal right to have access to a public school campus? It is possible that such a set of facts might exist, but it is not likely.

However, if the school has set a precedent of opening its facilities for use by the general public and other groups without qualifications, then the school cannot exclude religious groups from using those facilities.[19] Rarely would this kind of use of facilities exist during instructional time. However, it may occur before or after school hours if groups are given opportunities to speak on the campus.

Also, when a school has an athletic or other event that is open to the public, the exclusion of youth leaders would be unlawful. Therefore, youth leaders should take advantage of all opportunities to access the campus during such public events.

HOW TO RESPOND TO THE LAW

From this chapter we can draw these conclusions.

1. *The youth worker has no legal right to be on the public school campus.*

2. *Students have every legal right to express their faith as long as it doesn't vio-*

late another student's rights or disrupt the educational process.

3. Students can meet on campus to express their religious views as long as the meeting is student-initiated and student-led.

Youth workers are finding access to the public school campus increasingly difficult to obtain, despite the fact that the Supreme Court has affirmed the rights of students and teachers to express their religious views, and despite the passage of the Equal Access Act, which has given additional protection to students who wish to meet for prayer and Bible study.

In light of this trend, people involved in student ministries must learn to be flexible. They must think of new and creative strategies for gaining access to the public school campus and maximizing their student contacts.

On occasion school administrators may have violated the rights of youth workers, students, or teachers. Such instances are rare, but they can and do occur. If possible, those situations should be resolved peacefully with the school administration. If those efforts fail, the youth worker should suggest contacting legal counsel who specializes in the area of religious liberty.

Even though rights may be violated, it is preferable that such confrontations be avoided if at all possible. In most cases they can be avoided if the youth worker is not seen by the administration or by non-Christian students as an aggressor.

Our natural reaction when someone tells us that we have no rights is to fight back. To our great detriment, that response is emerging as a popular strategy for confronting authority on the public campuses. That is the wrong course of action, because youth leaders have no rights on the campus, and the students already have their rights. Any confrontation, then, becomes an attempt to carry our agendas onto the campus in the name of "standing up for Jesus!" We end up negating the attitude and approach of Jesus, who told us to lay down our lives and our rights in order to love those who revile and persecute us.

Instead, cultivate an aggressive attitude of patience and peaceableness that does not react to the challenges and threats of hostile school personnel. This can be accomplished if we project the image of a servant. The youth minister should do everything in his power to establish a good rapport with the school administration by demonstrating his desire to assist the school in their educational mission. You can accomplish this by following the approach described in this book.

When youth workers build their ministry on relationships rather than on rights, then they will have access to the campus, which in turn leads to changed lives. When youth leaders take this approach enough times in enough places, then not only will individual schools change, but they will also raise up a new generation of young people who will serve as the salt and light on their campuses to change our nation and the world.

> **When we build our ministry on relationships rather than on rights, then we will have access to the campus, which in turn leads to changed lives.**

If for some reason you need further or more detailed information about the legal aspects of campus ministry, we recommend that you:

- Read *Students' Legal Rights on a Public School Campus,* J.W. Brinkley, Roever Communications. For more information call (817) 238-2005.
- Contact The American Center of Law and Justice, P.O. Box 64429, Virginia Beach, VA 23467. For more information call (757) 226-2489 www.aclj.org.
- Read *A Guide to the Equal Access Act,* Center for Law and Religious Freedom, 4208 Evergreen Lane Suite 222, Annandale, VA 22003. For more information call (703) 642-1070 ext 350; www.christianlegalsociety.org

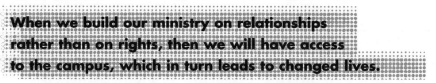

TAKING ACTION

A Strategy Regarding Legal Rights in Campus Ministry

1. From the legal information in the chapter, state what the law allows you to do as a youth worker.

_____

_____

_____

2. What does the law not allow you to do?

_____

_____

_____

3. What does the law allow students to do?

_____

_____

4. What does the law not allow students to do?

_____

_____

_____

5. What does the law allow teachers to do?

_____

_____

_____

6. What does the law not allow teachers to do?

_____

_____

_____

7. In a sentence or two, articulate your philosophy and approach to the legal issues on your campus(es) and how you will instruct your students and teachers.

_____

_____

_____

_____

_____

_____

8. If you run into a legal problem, what resources will be most helpful to you to solve that problem in a peaceable, Christ-like manner?

_____

_____

_____

_____

NOTES

1. Because of the nature of this work and space constraints, the treatment given to this subject is not exhaustive. This chapter is not designed to answer every question that can arise. Readers should also know that the law in this area is not static. The interpretation of applicable law can change, and principles can be modified under different circumstances. Also, legislatures can pass new laws which can alter the status quo. Therefore, anyone reading this chapter should contact counsel in the event questions arise. No one should rely solely on the text of this chapter to answer a complex legal question

2. The constitutional law of the fifty states can vary, so long as those state laws do not infringe on the protection granted by the United States Constitution.

3. The validity of this test is at issue in *Weisman v. Lee*, 728 F'.Supp. 68 (D.RI. 1991), affirmed 908 F.2d 1090 (1st Cir. 1991), cert. granted 111 S.Ct. 1305(1991). The Supreme Court has heard the arguments in this case and is due to render an opinion as this book goes to press.

4. *McCollum v. Board of Education*, 333 U.S. 203 (1948)

5. *Engel v. Vitale*, 370 U.S. 421 (1962)

6. *Abington School District v. Schempp*, 374 U.S. 203 (1963)

7. *Stone v. Graham*, 449 U.S. 39 (1980)

8. *Wallace v. Jaffree*, 472 U.S. 38 (1985)

9. 343 U.S. 306 (1952)

10. 393 U.S. 502 (1969)

11. 393 U.S. at 513

12. *Bender v. Williams Port Area School District*, 475 U.S. 534 (1986). See also Healy v. James, 408 U.S. 169 (1972).

13. 393 U.S. at 506

14. See *James v. Board of Education*, 461 F.2d 566 (2nd Cir.) cert. den 409 U.S. 1042 (1972), reh. den, 410 U.S. 947 (1973). In that case the court held that the First Amendment protected a high school teacher who wore a black armband to protest the Vietnam War. The teacher was a member of the Quaker faith.

15. *James v. Board of Education*, 461 F.2d at 573. See also, Bishop v.Aronov, 926 F.2d 1066 (11th Cir. 1991).

16. 20 U.S.C. ss 4071.4074. A copy of the Equal Access Act is included as an appendix

17. See *Lubbock Civil Liberties Union v. Lubbock Independent School District* 669 F.2d 1038 (5th Cir.1982), cert. den 459 U.S. 1155.1156 (1983); Brandon v. Board of Education of Guilderland Cent. Sch., 635 F.2d 971 (2nd Cir. 1980), cert. den 454 U.S. 1123 (1981).

18. 496 U.S. 226 (1990)

19. See *Widmar v. Vincent*, 454 U.S. 263 (1982); *Perry Education Assn. v. Perry Local Educators'Assn.*, 460 U.S. 37(1983); *Hazelwood School District v. Kuhlmeier*, 484 U.S. 260 (1988).

DISCUSSION GUIDES

If you lead a discussion of one of the chapters in *Penetrating the Campus*, use the appropriate discussion guide to help you get started. These questions and exercises will help you get to the heart of each chapter. Feel free, however, to add your own questions, ideas, and applications as well. Use this format to design your meeting:

Personal: What's going on in your life this week?

Projects: What did you discover this week? Discuss the assignment using the questions below.

Problems: What are your questions, struggles, or problems with applying this information?

Prayer: What do you want to pray for?

CHAPTER 1

1. Describe one student you know who is harassed, helpless, and like a sheep without a shepherd.

2. What evidence of desperation do you see on your campus?

3. Why do you think youth workers are reluctant to minister actively on their local campuses?

4. What experiences—either negative or positive—have you had with campus ministry?

5. From the discussion of Matthew 9:35-38 in this chapter, what did you discover that caused you to rethink your attitudes toward ministering on the campus?

CHAPTER 2

1. When have your efforts in ministry fallen short because of a failure to love a person or group of people unconditionally? Give one specific example.

2. Why do you think it is so important to keep your "channel of love" flowing freely?

3. As you apply having a pure heart, a good conscience, and a genuine faith to yourself, describe one issue that you personally need to deal with. How have you or will you deal with it?

CHAPTER 3

1. When have you experienced times of "extraordinary prayer" in your life?
2. On a scale from 1 to 10, where are we in our need for desperate prayer?
3. Identify or describe one barrier that keeps 2 Chronicles 7:14 from becoming a reality to you.
4. Describe your personal "Campus Prayer Strategy" in detail.
5. When revival comes, what will it look like? Identify four or five characteristics.

CHAPTER 4

1. Work on "A Strategy to Know the School" step by step, reporting what you have learned.
2. Pray for the school, using the information you have learned as the basis for your prayers.

CHAPTER 5

1. Divide into two groups, giving one group Romans 13:1-5 and the other group Ephesians 6:5-9. Discuss the principle of submission and its application to the campus. Why is developing a submissive attitude so important for a successful campus ministry?
2. As a group, talk through each person's strategy with the school administration, then come up with a comprehensive approach.

CHAPTER 6

1. Why is serving others such a struggle for us? Be specific.
2. Let's share our prayers, asking God to make us servants.
3. What is your creative serving strategy with students? Let each person tell what he or she plans to do. If your time is limited, you may want to divide the group into smaller units for this discussion.
4. Close this session by washing each other's feet as a symbol of our desire to serve young people. Read John 13:1-17, then wash the first person's feet; that person then washes the next person's feet; and so on. Close in prayer.

CHAPTER 7

1. Share the one sentence mission statement you will take with you to the campus.
2. Describe the one group of students you want to get to know.
3. To what groups of people do you tend to show favoritism? In what ways do you

need to work on loving other people?

4. Share the names of three non-Christian students you want to reach. Describe each one. Then break into groups and pray for each one.

CHAPTER 8

1. In teams of two, go through each step of "A Practical Plan to Share the Message of Christ."

2. Remain in these teams and role play a conversation from start to finish. One person should play himself (the youth leader) while the other person plays a student. Then switch roles and do the role play again.

3. Pray for the students with whom you have an appointment.

CHAPTER 9

1. In the past how much importance have you attached to following up with new Christians?

2. What felt needs do you see in the lives of new believers at your school?

3. How would you respond to a student who asked you, "How can I tell my friends about my faith in Jesus?"

4. In what specific ways would you help a new Christian get plugged in at your church?

CHAPTER 10

1. Developing an effective follow-up strategy is very important not only for our youth group, but also for the young people in this community. Let's do an honest evaluation of our youth ministry and determine what we need to do differently.

2. To create the right environment to mobilize students, let's decide what we need to do:
- in our own personal evangelism
- in our prayer with other youth leaders
- in mobilizing our young people into prayer triplets
- in balancing our youth ministry activities

Together work through "The Youth Ministry Process" sheet. Agree together on what you need to do.

3. To implement a plan that trains students to reach their friends, what do we need to change about our discipleship ministry?

4. To create a movement of students to reach the campus what do we need to do.

- in ongoing local opportunities?
- in short-term mission trips?
- for total campus penetration?

Because this list is so comprehensive, you may want to set up extra meetings or divide the group into four smaller groups, having each one discuss a specific area. Then reassemble the group and put all the information together.

CHAPTER 11

1. Let's evaluate our current status in campus ministry training. (As appropriate, take your group through the "Taking Action" section, evaluating each aspect: model, motivate, mobilize, and multiply.)

2. What specific steps of action do we need to take now to get to the goal of establishing a ministry on every campus within our sphere of influence? Identify specific leaders and specific campuses.

3. Let's pray for God to expand our vision and to focus our strategy for reaching every campus.

CHAPTER 12

1. What misconceptions did you have about youth workers' rights on the school campus before reading this chapter?

2. What rights do students, teachers, and youth leaders have on the campus?

3. Let's work on a one-paragraph statement that will state our particular approach to the legal aspects of the campus. (Work on this together.)

4. Reflect on the specifics of what the Lord has taught you during these weeks. Let's pray for each other and for God to impact the campuses in our community with the life-changing message of Jesus.

THE EQUAL ACCESS ACT

SUBCHAPTER VIII-EQUAL ACCESS

ß407 1 Denial of equal access prohibited

(a)Restriction of limited open forum on basis of religious, political, philosophical, or other speech content prohibited
It shall be unlawful for any public secondary school which receives federal financial assistance and which has a limited open forum to deny equal access or a fair opportunity to, or discriminate against, any students who wish to conduct a meeting within that limited open forum on the basis of the religious, political, philosophical, or other content of the speech at such meetings.

(b)"Limited open forum" defined
A public secondary school has a limited open forum whenever such school grants an offering to or opportunity for one or more non-curriculum related student groups to meet on school premises during non-instructional time.

(c) Fair opportunity criteria
Schools shall be deemed to offer a fair opportunity to students who wish to conduct a meeting within its limited open forum if such school uniformly provides that-
(1) the meeting is voluntary and student-initiated;
(2) there is no sponsorship of the meeting by the school, the government, or its agents or employees;
(3) employees or agents of the school or government are present at religious meetings only in a non-participatory capacity;
(4) the meeting does not materially and substantially interfere with the orderly conduct of educational activities within the school; and
(5) non-school persons may not direct, conduct, control, or regularly attend activities of student groups.

(d) Federal or State authority nonexistent with respect to certain rights

Nothing in this subchapter shall be construed to authorize the United States or any State or political subdivision thereof-

(1) to influence the form or content of any prayer or other religious activity;

(2) to require any person to participate in prayer or other religious activity;

(3) to expend public funds beyond the incidental cost of providing the space for student-initiated meetings;

(4) to compel any school agent or employee to attend a school meeting if the content of the speech at the meeting is contrary to the beliefs of the agent or employee;

(5) to sanction meetings that are otherwise unlawful;

(6) to limit the rights of groups of students which are not of a specified numerical size; or

(7) to abridge the constitutional rights of any person.

(e) Unaffected Federal financial assistance to schools
Notwithstanding the availability of any other remedy under the Constitution or the laws of the United States, nothing in this subchapter shall be construed to authorize the United States to deny or withhold Federal financial assistance to any school.

(I) Authority of schools with respect to order-and-discipline, well-being, and voluntary-presence concerns
Nothing in this subchapter shall be construed to limit the authority of the school, its agents or employees, to maintain order and discipline on school premises, to protect the well-being of students and faculty, and to assure that attendance of students at meetings is voluntary.

HISTORICAL AND STATUTORY NOTES

2. Generally

Equal Access Act does not require school district to permit unconstitutional use of school property and thus because under Washington's Constitution, meetings of religious groups on school premises would introduce sectarian influences into school and result in impermissible appropriation of public money on property for religious purposes in violation of the State Constitution, mandatory provisions of Equal Access Act were not triggered. *Garnett v. Renton School Dist No. 403,* W.D.Wash. 1987, 675 F.Supp. 1268.

Equal Access Act ~Equal Access Act, ßß802-805, 20 U.S.C.A. ßß4071- 40741 was not applicable to question of whether school district could deny access to facilities to non-curriculum-related student group which intended to invite general public to antinuclear rally and peace exposition where it had not been policy or practice of school to indiscriminately permit use of facilities in question to other non-curriculum-related student groups which desired to invite non-students/the general public. *Student Coalition for Peace v. Lower Merion School Dist*, D.C.Pa.1985, 618 F.Supp. 53.

3. Limited open forum

Because public high school was not a limited First Amendment public forum, Equal Access Act did not require that it make classroom available to a group of religious students who wish to meet prior to the beginning of the school day. *Garnet By and Through Smith v. Renton School Dist. No. 403*, CA.9 (Wash.) 1989, 874 F.2d 608.

Public secondary schools' sponsorship of non-curriculum-related student clubs rendered school a "limited open forum" and required school, under Equal Access Act, to allow students to form a Christian Bible study club to meet at school. Mergens By and *Through Mergens v. Board of Educ. of Westside Community Schools (Dist 66')*, C.A.8 (Neb.) 1989,867 F.2d 1076.

Public high school did not have "limited open forum," as defined by the Equal Access Act, and school was accordingly not required by mandatory provisions of the Act to allow student religious group to hold meetings in school classroom prior to start of school day; all school clubs directly related to high school curriculum as defined by school district *Garnet By and Through Smith v. Renton School Dist No. 403*, C.A.9 (Wash.) 1989, 865 F.2d 1121.

In order to establish right to use school athletic field for peace exposition under the Equal Access Act, ß802 et seq., 20 U.S.C.A. ß4071 et seq., which provides that it is unlawful for public secondary school receiving federal financing and having limited open forum to deny students to equal access to forum, student organization would be required to prove that school board's policy or practice after effective date of the Act with respect to noncurricular student groups created a limited open forum broad enough to include contemplated use. *Student Coalition for Peace v. Lower Merion School Dist Bd. of School Directors*, C.A.3 (Pa.) 1985, 776 F.2d

431, on remand 633 F.Supp. 1040.

School created limited open forum within meaning of Equal Access Act by allowing non-curriculum-related student clubs to meet on school premises during non-instructional time. *Thompson by Thompson v. Waynesboro Area School Dist.*, M.D.Pa. 1987, 673 F.Supp. 1379.

Equal Access Act would not be applied to allow religious meetings at high school as "limited open forums," where that application would override establishment clause interests of school district *Clark v. Dallas Independent School Dist.*, N.D.Tex.1987, 671 F.Supp. 1119, amended 701 F.Supp. 594.

Under Equal Access Act, school district could not prohibit use of high school gym by non-school-sponsored student organization which sought to conduct public anti-nuclear exposition, where school district had previously granted permission to use gym for a volleyball marathon, thereby creating limited open forum. *Student Coalition for Peace v. Lower Merion School Dist Bd. of School Directors*, E.D.Pa1986, 633 F.Supp. 1040.

4. Nonstudent participation

The Equal Access Act, ß802(c), 20 U.S.C.A. ß4071(c), which states that school does not violate equal access requirement by providing that non-students may not direct, conduct, control or regularly attend activities of student groups wishing to invite non-students onto school property be protected by Act if school's limited open forum encompasses non-student participation in student events, as long as those non-students do not direct, conduct, control or regularly attend such activities, but school is not required to permit any and all outsiders to use its facilities, or even to permit student groups indiscriminately to invite outsiders to its activities. *Student Coalition for Peace v. Lower Merion School Dist. Bd. of School Directors*, C.A.3 (Pa.) 1985, 776 F.2d 431, on remand 633 F.Supp. 1040.

5. Injunction

School organization could maintain private cause of action for injunction ordering school board to permit organization to use school property for peace exposition, under the Equal Access Act, ß802 et seq., 20 U.S.C.A. ß407 1 et seq., which provides that public secondary school receiving federal financial assistance shall not deny students equal access to limited open forum, since the Act created mandatory duties but provided no express means of enforcing them. *Student Coalition for Peace v. Lower Merion School Dist Bd. of School Directors*, C.A.3 (Pa.) 1985, 776 F.2d 431, on remand 633 F.Supp. 1040.

6. Purpose

The Equal Access Act, ß802 et seq., 20 U.S.C.A. ß4071 et seq., which provides that it is unlawful for public secondary school receiving federal financial assistance to deny students equal access to limited open forum, was intended to create judicially enforceable duties and corresponding rights. *Student Coalition for Peace v. Lower Merion School Dist. Bd. of School Directors*, C.A.3 (Pa.) 1985,776 F.2d 431, on remand 633 F.Supp. 1040.

By enacting Equal Access Act, Congress sought to prohibit denial of non-curricular-related student groups' meetings on basis of subject matter, namely as to religious, political, philosophical, or other content of the speech; thus, Congress afforded students right to use school property beyond constitutional guarantees in First Amendment. *Student Coalition for Peace v. Lower Merion School Dist. Bd. of Directors*, E.D.Pa.1986, 633 F.Supp. 1040.

ß4072. Definitions

As used in this subchapter-

(1) The term "secondary school" means a public school which provides secondary education as determined by State law.

(2) The term "sponsorship" includes the act of promoting, leading, or participating in a meeting. The assignment of a teacher, administrator, or other school employee to a meeting for custodial purposes does not constitute sponsorship of the meeting.

(3) The term "meeting" includes those activities of student groups which are permitted under a school's limited open forum and are not directly related to the school curriculum.

(4) The term "non-instructional time" means time set aside by the school before actual classroom instruction begins or after actual classroom instruction ends.